Islamic Economics Series – 15

Islam, Poverty and Income Distribution

A discussion of the distinctive Islamic approach to eradication of poverty and achievement of an equitable distribution of income and wealth

ZIAUDDIN AHMAD

The Islamic Foundation

ISBN 086037-212-X (HB)
ISBN 086037-213-8 (PB)

Views expressed by different writers represent their personal views and do not necessarily represent the views of the Islamic Foundation.

Cover design: Anwar Cara

Published by
The Islamic Foundation,
Markfield Dawah Centre,
Ratby Lane, Markfield,
Leicester, UK.

Quran House,
P.O. Box 30611,
Nairobi,
Kenya.

P.M.B. 3193,
Kano,
Nigeria.

British Library Cataloguing in Publication Data

Ahmad, Ziauddin
Islam, poverty and income distribution. –
(Islamic economics series; 15)
I. Title II. Series
330.0917671

ISBN 0-86037-212-X
ISBN 0-86037-213-8 pbk

Printed and bound by
Cromwell Press Ltd., Broughton Gifford, Wiltshire

بسم الله الرحمن الرحيم

Contents

Foreword 5

Preface 11

Introduction 13

Chapter 1: Islamic Vision of a Just Socio-Economic Order 15

Chapter 2: Policy Framework for Eradication of Poverty and Achievement of an Equitable Distribution of Income and Wealth 25

Encouragement of Productive Effort 25

Adoption of an Islamically-Oriented Growth Strategy 27

Regulation of Business Practices 30

Equality of Opportunity 31

Property Rights and Obligations in Islam 32

Inheritance Laws 34

Factor Shares and Functional Distribution of Income 36

Encouragement of Voluntary Spending for the Welfare of the Poor 42

Fiscal and Monetary Policies 44

Islam's Social Security System 47

Chapter 3: The Distinctiveness of the Islamic Approach 61

Chapter 4: Summary and Conclusions 95

Glossary 99

Bibliography 101

Index 109

Foreword

> Oh Lord! I seek Thy refuge from infidelity (*kufr*), and from poverty and destitution (*faqr*) . . . and seek Thy refuge from paucity (*qillah*) and humiliation (*dhillah*).
>
> Prophet Muḥammad (peace be upon him)

If there exists a mirror to reflect *par excellence* the most sublime and the most cherished in the hierarchy of values one enshrines, prayer is such a mirror. Prayer represents the ladder that connects what is with what ought to be. It provides a vivid peep into a person's vision of the good and the desirable. This is as true about a religion and a community, as it is for the individual. The spirit of Islam and of its historical ethos can be understood by a close examination of the prayers made by the prophets of Allah, as given in the Qur'ān and the *Sunnah*.

The prayer quoted above represents one of the prayers sought by the Prophet Muḥammad (peace be upon him). It epitomizes the distinct Islamic approach to the challenges humanity has faced from time immemorial. Denial of the Lord and recourse to a purely materialistic and secular approach represent one aspect of this challenge; failure to cater for the basic physical needs of man on the earth represents the other. It is folly to regard these two as separate entities. Failure to appreciate the link between the two has resulted in historic catastrophes yesterday and today. Humanity was left to be wrapped in religions that ignored the challenges of poverty and deprivation. Secular ideologies, at the other end of the spectrum, tried to grapple with problems of poverty while ignoring altogether the religious and the moral dimension.

The uniqueness of Islam lies in resurrecting the link

between the two in a manner that the spiritual and the material become two aspects of the same reality, shading into each other, one inseparable from the other, in fact each determining the character and the fortune of the other.

The Qur'ān says:

> Have you seen him who denies the Religion?
> It is he who harshly repels the orphan
> and does not urge others to feed the needy.
>
> (107: 1–2)

In the Qur'ānic paradigm failure to fulfil the needs of the poor and the orphans amounts to denial of religion and of the Day of Judgement. Worship, on the other hand, is a natural response to what Allah has done for mankind. Protecting people from hunger and ensuring security of life and honour are essential elements of the social order man is entitled to in the world. The Qur'ān says:

> Let them worship the Lord of this House, Who provides them with food lest they should go hungry, and with security lest they should live in fear.
>
> (106: 3–4)

That is why the Prophet (peace be upon him) is reported to have said that *faqr* (poverty and destitution) have the propensity to lead one towards *kufr* (infidelity and rebellion against religion). The significance of the above prayer lies in highlighting the link between infidelity and poverty, paucity and humiliation. This also brings into sharp focus the foundations of an Islamic socio-economic policy, characterized on the one hand by purification of the soul, inculcating within man the motive to be 'loyal to God and to be good to His creatures' and on the other so organizing the society, its institutions and policies, as to eradicate poverty and establish justice. If the hallmark of capitalist economics is a search for efficiency, the distinctive approach of Islamic economics lies in establishing the primacy of justice and equity in a manner that efficiency and growth become a means to this end.

The economic achievements of the industrial civilization, now dominant over most of the globe, are not in dispute. Yet, it also remains indisputable that despite almost three centuries of industrial and technological revolutions, poverty and destitution could not be wiped off the face of the earth. The latest *World Development Report, The Challenge of Development 1991* (World Bank, Oxford University Press, 1991) laments that around forty per cent of the human race lives below the poverty line. Even the most advanced countries of the world, capitalist and socialist alike, cannot claim that hunger and poverty have been eliminated from the paradise they have built. This is a sad commentary on the ideologies and strategies pursued in the economic realm over the last several centuries.

Muslim economists are trying to look upon the problems of poverty and inequality from a perspective different from the one economists and policy-makers are familiar with in the Western world. Departing from a purely secular approach, they are trying to face this challenge by drawing upon the rich spiritual and religious tradition of Islam.

This new approach gives equal importance to the spiritual and moral as well as the material and physical factors that influence man's motives and behaviour patterns. Its focus is simultaneously on the individual and the socio-economic framework in which he operates. It is neither obsessed with market mechanism to an extent that it is not prepared to acknowledge the healthy and positive role the government and its policies can play in economic life, nor has it any doctrinaire love for an all-pervading state that so regulates the economy that economic freedom is subsumed by state regimentation.

Dr. Ziauddin Ahmad's present study, *Islam, Poverty and Income Distribution,* is an original and path-breaking contribution to literature on development economics in general and on Islamic economics in particular. He has breathed some fresh air into a debate that was becoming stale and somewhat insipid. He has shown how, by drawing upon the Islamic sources, a modern state can strike at the roots of the problems of poverty, exploitation and inequality.

Dr. Ziauddin Ahmad is a leading Pakistani economist who

has played an important role in the development of central banking in the country. Educated at Harvard, he rose to the distinguished positions of Economic Advisor and then Deputy Governor of the State Bank of Pakistan. His seminal contribution, however, lies in evolving an interest-free model of economy for Pakistan. As convenor of the Panel of Economists and Bankers and also as an active member of the Council for Islamic Ideology he played a pioneering role in developing an Islamic economic programme in the late 1970s and early 1980s in Pakistan. As the first Director General of the International Institute for Islamic Economics, International Islamic University, he made a signal contribution in developing an integrated teaching and research programme in Islamic economics for undergraduate and post-graduate levels. During the last fifteen years, he has played a very significant role in the development of the nascent discipline of Islamic economics. His many papers on different aspects of Islamic banking have been a source of inspiration and light. His new treatise, *Islam, Poverty and Income Distribution,* breaks fresh ground and shows how Islam can answer humanity's call to eradicate poverty and establish a social order based on justice for all.

Islam, Poverty and Income Distribution is an authentic exposition of the Islamic approach to the eradication of poverty. It is also rich in ideas, rigorous in analysis, and innovative in suggestions and prescriptions. In my view, this study is important for a number of reasons.

Firstly, the author has expounded, in clear and candid terms, the socio-economic objectives of an Islamic economy in the contemporary context and consequent policy options. This exposition goes beyond general statements of goals and objectives; it delineates a comprehensive policy framework for the elimination of poverty, identifying specific policy instruments capable of eradicating this menace. The analysis takes into account the major causes of poverty and the policy prescription outlined goes a long way in suggesting how these causes could be eliminated. The author also shows how this approach is different from the approaches adopted under capitalism and socialism. As such this study provides very valuable guidelines for planners and policy-makers in the Muslim world.

Secondly, this study has beautifully encapsulated the multi-dimensional approach that Islam brings to bear upon the problems of human society. Capitalism and socialism have made distinct contributions in *some* specific fields and have blundered in others, primarily by adopting an almost one-dimensional approach. Islam, on the other hand, adopts an approach that is comprehensive enough to simultaneously cover different aspects of individual and social life. The present study shows that eradication of poverty is possible if a more comprehensive approach is adopted, starting with human motivation, leading to the development of a framework that is capable of simultaneously addressing itself to problems associated with property, economic rights, private enterprise, profit motive, just wage, variable return on capital, market mechanism, social security, income distribution and state intervention and guidance. Dr. Ziauddin Ahmad has shown how a comprehensive policy-mix can be developed by seeking guidance from the Islamic sources. The message comes out clearly: the menace of poverty cannot be tackled unless the questions of human motivation, limits to profit motive and market mechanism, issues relating to the distribution of income and wealth and the shape of the monetary, fiscal and welfare policies of the state are tackled simultaneously. It is only in such a multi-dimensional milieu that this problem can be solved. In a word, it is only by relating *every* aspect of economic activity and behaviour to the core concept of *justice* that this challenge can be faced.

Thirdly, the author has come up with some concrete ideas about change of institutions and development of new policy tools which deserve to be considered very carefully. Among others I would like to emphasize special consideration to his plea for the revival of the institution of *ḥisbah* in the economy, the suggestion about the promotion of micro-entrepreneurship, the need for investment in education and health, the idea of restructuring the national budget into an administrative-cum-development budget and welfare budget, and the need for evolving an unemployment insurance policy which is not just unemployment-compensatory but positively employment-generating.

Finally, to the students and researchers in Islamic

economics also this study has a message. Without in any way discounting the importance of and the need for the elimination of *ribā* and introduction of *zakāh,* this study brings into sharp focus the need for looking upon these aspects within the total framework of Islamic economics. The importance of this study lies in highlighting the framework and not just some of its elements. There is an urgent need for directing more research efforts towards developing a deeper understanding of the nature and problems of the general framework and its inter-relationships, so as to develop more rigorously a general theory of Islamic economics.

Leicester
3 Muharram 1412 A.H.
15 July 1991

Khurshid Ahmad

Preface

Islam is as much concerned with the welfare of man in this world as with his salvation in the Hereafter. It is unfortunate that so many Muslim countries are afflicted with widespread poverty and gross inequalities of income and wealth while Islamic teachings provide the most effective guidelines for eradicating poverty and achieving an equitable distribution of income and wealth. The ongoing Islamic resurgence gives cause for hope that Islamic teachings will be put into practice in Muslim countries before long. There is much in Islamic teachings which is of general application, and the Islamic approach to issues of poverty and income distribution deserves to be more widely known. I hope this publication will be of wide general interest.

The exposition in the book represents my own understanding of how Islam seeks to eradicate poverty and achieve an equitable distribution of income and wealth. The chief sources of knowledge on the subject have of course been the Qur'ān, the *Sunnah* and *Fiqh* literature, but in developing the theme of the book, I have benefited from the writings of many scholars too numerous to be mentioned by name. However, material which has been specially helpful has been acknowledged in the text and the footnotes.

This study was completed during my tenure as a consultant to the Middle-Eastern Department of the International Monetary Fund, Washington during 1989–90. I am grateful to the Fund for the permission accorded for its publication by the Islamic Foundation.

Subsequent to my separation from the Fund, I have received some comments on the study from Dr. M.N. Siddiqi, Dr. M.U. Chapra and Professor Volker Nienhaus. I have greatly benefited from the observations made by them and have improved the presentation in certain parts of the study in the light of some of these observations. I am, however, alone responsible for any deficiencies that may still be found in the study.

I am grateful to Dr. Abdelkader Chachi of the Islamic Foundation for the assistance provided to me in finalizing some of the footnotes of the study. Credit is also due to Mr. E.R. Fox for technical editing and seeing the book through the press.

Leicester,
1 Muharram, 1412 A.H.
13 July, 1991

Ziauddin Ahmad

Introduction

The Islamic approach to eradication of poverty and achievement of an equitable distribution of income and wealth is part of an overall scheme for the establishment of a just socio-economic order. Islam attaches great importance to the dignity of each individual human being. It, therefore, stands for the banishment of poverty and organization of economic life in a manner that the basic needs of all human beings are met. Since Islam is opposed to regimentation, it seeks to achieve this purpose through influencing the behaviour pattern of the members of the society in particular directions and activation of a number of institutional mechanisms duly supplemented by suitable state action. Islam stands for the abolition of all class distinctions and equal regard for all human beings. This does not, however, call for the obliteration of all inequalities of income and wealth. In fact, inequalities serving a functional purpose are held to be fully justifiable. Nevertheless, the general thrust of Islamic teachings is toward the establishment of a fairly egalitarian society.

This book seeks to delineate the Islamic position on issues of poverty and income distribution. The first chapter outlines the Islamic vision of a just socio-economic order with particular reference to distributive justice. The second chapter sets out the broad contours of the policy framework provided by Islam for the eradication of poverty and achievement of an equitable distribution of income and wealth. The third chapter seeks to bring out the distinctive features of the Islamic approach to issues of poverty and income distribution compared to certain other systemic approaches. The final chapter summarizes the main contents of the book.

CHAPTER 1

Islamic Vision of a Just Socio-Economic Order

Islam enjoins justice in all matters affecting human society. The basic teachings of Islam are contained in the Qur'ān[1] and the *Sunnah*.[2] The early Islamic period[3] provides vivid illustrations of practical implementation of these teachings. The Islamic vision of a just socio-economic order can be deduced with reference to these basic teachings and the historical record of the early Islamic period.

According to the Qur'ān, the basic purpose of the guidance provided by God through His messengers is to enable mankind to establish justice.[4] God has made man His vicegerent on earth,[5] and enjoined on him the duty of dealing justly with everyone.[6] No subject is more closely connected with the concept of justice than 'human rights'. The first source of Islamic law *(sharī'ah)*, the Qur'ān, laid down the fundamental elements of a charter of human rights which have the binding force of both a moral obligation and a legal system. These are supplemented by the second source of Islamic law, the Prophet's sayings and actions, known as *Sunnah*. Combined, they hold the promise of eliminating all forms of exploitation, oppression, and injustice.[7]

All the human rights granted by Islam are based on the principle of 'general good' *(al-maṣlaḥah al-'āmmah)*. The rights which have a specific bearing on the subject matter of this study may be listed as follows:

a. Right to life. Human life is sacred and inviolable, and every effort shall be made to protect it.

b. Freedom of profession. There should be free entry into all professions which are permitted in Islam.

c. All persons are equal before the law and entitled to redress their grievances in accordance with *sharī'ah*.

d. Every person is entitled to own property individually or in association with others. State ownership of certain economic resources in the public interest is legitimate.

e. The poor have a right in the wealth of the rich to the extent that the basic needs of everyone in society are met.

f. Human exploitation at any level in any shape under any circumstances is anti-Islamic and must be ended.

Distributive justice is one of the most important components of the Islamic vision of a just socio-economic order. The most noteworthy feature of the scheme of distributive justice as envisaged by Islam is the assurance of the fulfilment of the basic needs of all, irrespective of the stage of development of a country. This implies the complete eradication of what is known as 'absolute poverty' in the current economic literature. The second aspect of distributive justice has to do with the general pattern of income distribution in society. Here the Islamic view is more flexible in that the guidelines in respect to the desired pattern of income and wealth distribution contained in the Qur'ān and the *Sunnah* are couched in general terms and allow for a great deal of latitude in dealing with this matter.

Islamic insistence on the fulfilment of the basic needs of all human beings is to be seen in the perspective of the Islamic view of man's place in the universe. God, the Qur'ān declares, has honoured the progeny of Adam and has made provision of good things for them.[8] Man is the vicegerent of God on earth, and it is his duty therefore to so arrange the affairs of the world that all have their due share in the 'good things' of life. God has provided all necessary resources for the fulfilment of the basic needs of mankind, and whatever has been created in the heavens and on earth has been made subservient to man.[9] These resources have been created by Him as a gift to mankind as a whole and whatever comes into the possession of any single individual is to be treated as a 'trust'.[10] This trust cannot be said to have been duly discharged unless each and every one has enough to satisfy at least his basic needs.

Islamic religious belief emphasizes the transitory nature of man's life on this earth and urges man to do good deeds for salvation in the Hereafter. However, it is firmly opposed to renunciation of this world to earn merit in the Hereafter.[11] The Qur'ān clearly states that God desires ease for mankind and not hardship.[12] The sayings of the Prophet also make it abundantly clear that poverty and deprivation are not a commendable virtue in Islam, and every effort should be made to eliminate them.[13]

To ensure the fulfilment of the basic needs of all, Islam enunciates the principle of the poor having a 'right' *(ḥaqq)* in the income and wealth of the well-off members of the society.[14] According to Islam, humanity is a single creation of God, and all have an equal right to acquire their sustenance from God-given resources. However, if, for whatever reason, some members of the human brotherhood fail to acquire sufficient provision for the fulfilment of their basic needs through their own efforts, they have a right in the earnings and wealth of others.

Islam uses both moral exhortation and legal measures to eliminate poverty and deprivation so that the basic needs of all are duly fulfilled. A number of verses in the Qur'ān emphasize the virtue of *infāq,* that is, voluntary spending for the welfare of the poor. It is proclaimed, for example, that in no case will man attain piety unless he spends freely from his wealth in the way of God for the needy and the poor.[15] Those who practise *infāq* are promised the choicest of blessings in heaven. The Prophet set an example himself in liberal spending for the welfare of the poor.[16] He exhorted his followers to excel each other in helping the poor. He constantly reminded them that a society which fails to take care of the needs of the needy cannot be regarded as Islamic.[17] He also warned them that a locality in which one has to starve a night is forsaken by God.[18]

Islam is greatly concerned that the poor should be helped in such a way that their self respect is not hurt. The best way of helping a poor, unemployed person is considered to be the rendering of such assistance as enables him to become self supporting.[19] The Qur'ān exhorts people to go out and search for such persons who are in need but do not stretch out their hands to beg.[20] The Qur'ān also warns that charity becomes worthless in the eyes of God if it is followed by any action which hurts the feelings of the recipient.[21]

Islam recognizes that societies do not behave uniformly in living up to the moral precepts of religion. It, therefore, supplements moral exhortations to help the needy by a powerful social security system. It enjoins on the state the duty of collecting a compulsory levy known as *zakāh* from the well-to-do sections of the society whose proceeds are earmarked for specific purposes in which help to the needy figures most prominently.[22] This social security system was set up in the time of the Prophet and functioned effectively in the early Islamic period and for quite some time in the subsequent period.[23] In fact, recorded history shows that there were instances in this period when in certain regions no needy person could be found who was prepared to accept charity.[24]

The rulers in the early Islamic period were fully conscious of their responsibility in respect of the fulfilment of the basic needs of all citizens. The first four Caliphs who ruled the Muslim land after the death of the Prophet regarded need fulfilment as one of the basic objectives of state policy. In the period of the first Caliph, Abū Bakr, a section of the population refused to pay *zakāh*. Their refusal to pay *zakāh* was treated as an act of rebellion against the state and armed action was taken against them until they agreed to pay it. The second Caliph, 'Umar, was so acutely conscious of this responsibility that he declared: 'If a camel dies unattended on the banks of the Euphrates, I am afraid Allah would make me accountable for it.'[25]

Muslim jurists have written extensively on the principle of need fulfilment. They are all agreed that it is the collective duty of the society in general that none should remain deprived of the basic necessities of life. A number of jurists have held the view that legal protection should be afforded to the principle of need fulfilment so that any citizen could go to court to secure the implementation of this principle.[26]

The jurists have also discussed the important question of

the identification of basic needs which have to be met of all citizens. The Qur'ān and the *Sunnah* have repeatedly emphasized feeding of the hungry;[27] fulfilment of the nutritional requirements of everyone has, therefore, to figure most prominently in the alleviation of the hardship of the poor. Other basic needs whose fulfilment commands high priority are clothing and housing.[28] The jurists have pointed out that while food, clothing, and housing are necessary for bare survival there are certain other needs which should be taken care of in an Islamic society. The juristic literature draws a line of distinction between three types of human needs, classified as *ḍarūriyyāt* (necessities), *ḥājiyyāt* (conveniences), and *taḥsīniyyāt* (refinements).[29] Necessities are held to include not only items which safeguard *nafs* (man's physical existence) but also those which protect *dīn* (religion), *'aql* (intellect or reason), *nasl* (progeny) and *māl* (property). The *ḥājiyyāt* improve the quality of life and remove bearable hardship and difficulty while *taḥsīniyyāt* add beauty and elegance to life without transgressing the limits of moderation. It is the view of the jurists that it is the collective responsibility of the society to ensure the fulfilment of *ḍarūriyyāt* in any case and also of *ḥājiyyāt* if resources permit. It is recognized that because of changing circumstances, the delimitation of needs in the three above-mentioned categories cannot remain constant over time. What is important is that the guarantee of fulfilment of basic needs must be available to each individual, even though the exact determination of these basic needs and the extent to which the various constituents of basic needs can be satisfied at any particular time has to be decided in accordance with actual conditions and the average standard of living in a country.

Apart from eradication of absolute poverty and fulfilment of the basic needs of all human beings, the Islamic vision of a just socio-economic order also envisages an equitable pattern of income and wealth distribution. The Qur'ān and the *Sunnah* make it quite clear that Islam does not seek to obliterate all inequalities of income and wealth. In fact, it regards the existence of certain income differentials as part of God's scheme of things. The Qur'ān says that God has raised some above others in the matter of livelihood and social degrees so that 'some of them may utilize the services of others in their work'.[30] In other words, Islam regards certain income differentials to be necessary in the interests of the smooth functioning of the economy.

Islam strongly disapproves inequalities of income which arise from exploitative practices. However, it is not against income differentials which are generated in the course of honest pursuit of various types of permissible economic activities. The Qur'ān exhorts: 'Give full measure, and be not of those who give less (than the due)',[31] implying that people should get just compensation for their work commensurate with their skill and effort.

Though Islam is not opposed to the existence of certain income and wealth differentials in society, it disfavours prevalence of gross inequalities of income and wealth. The Qur'ān cautions against glaring inequalities in income and wealth in verse 59: 7 where it is said that wealth should not be allowed to become 'a commodity between the rich among you'. The Islamic teachings, whether related to personal behaviour or state policies, have a pronounced redistributive orientation. Social justice is an inalienable aspect of the Islamic faith, and gross inequalities of income and wealth cannot but be repugnant to its spirit.

It is noteworthy that as against the unswerving insistence on fulfilment of the basic needs of all human beings in all circumstances and at all times, Islam does not prescribe any rigid standard of income distribution to which all societies in all ages should necessarily conform. There is no concept of a ceiling on an individual's total wealth though norms of earning and spending wealth are clearly laid down. It seems that it is the intent of Islam that the acceptable level of income inequalities should be determined by the people themselves in the light of their own circumstances. Islam seeks to promote to the utmost the idea of interdependence of utility functions.[32] Islam also severely condemns the use of wealth for extravagant expenditures and conspicuous consumption.[33] Both of these reflect the social mores of a society and have a significant bearing on the level of acceptable inequalities. There can be no way of determining the optimality of income distribution unless enough is known about the social mores of a society. It can, however, be stated as a general proposition that the more a society is permeated by the spirit of *al-'adl* (justice) and *al-iḥsān* (benevolence), enjoined by the Qur'ān and the *Sunnah*, and the less the affluent sections of the population indulge in conspicuous consumption, the greater will be the community's tolerance of income and wealth inequalities. On the other hand, the more pronounced the sense of relative deprivation in sections of the population as a result of non-fulfilment of basic needs and conspicuous consumption by the rich, the lower will be the community's tolerance of inequalities. By showing utmost concern for the welfare of the poor through eradication of absolute poverty and by keeping income and wealth inequalities within acceptable limits, the early Islamic period gave a practical demonstration of the implementation of the Islamic vision of a just socio-economic order.

Notes and References

1. The Book consisting of revelations made by God to the Prophet Muḥammad. In all references to the Qur'ān in this book, the first number refers to the *sūrah* (chapter) and the second to the *āyah* (verses). The English rendering of the verses has been taken from the translations of Muhammad Marmaduke Pickthall and Abdullah Yusuf Ali.

2. The way of the Prophet comprising what he did or said or tacitly approved.

3. The early Islamic period, for purposes of this book, refers to the period of the Prophet and the first four Caliphs covering a time span of about half a century.

4. Qur'ān, 57: 25.

5. Qur'ān, 2: 30.

6. Qur'ān, 5: 8.

7. See Javid Iqbal, 'Human Rights in Islam', in *Islamic Law and Social and Economic Development* (Islamabad: Idarah Saqafat-e-Pakistan, n.d.).

8. 'Verily we have honoured the children of Adam. We carry them on the land and the sea, and have made provision of good things for them, and have preferred them above many of those whom We created with a marked preferment' (Qur'ān, 17: 70).

9. Qur'ān, 31: 20.

10. Qur'ān, 57: 7.

11. The Qur'ān says: 'But monasticism they invented, we ordained it not for them' (57: 27).

12. Qur'ān, 2: 185.

13. The Prophet is reported to have advised his followers: 'Seek Allah's refuge from poverty, scarcity, and ignominy.' See Ibn Mājah, *Sunan Ibn Mājah* (Riyadh: Sharikah at-Ṭibā'ah al-'Arabīyah as-Sa'ūdīyah, 1984), Vol. 2, p. 344.

14. Qur'ān, 70: 24–5; 51: 19.

15. Qur'ān, 3: 92.

16. It is reported that the Prophet hardly kept anything for himself and his family beyond the bare subsistence requirements, and helped the poor and the needy to the utmost. For an account of the austere style of his living and his benevolence to others, see Muḥammad Ḥusayn Haykal, *The Life of Muhammad* (North American Trust Publications, 1976), pp. 185–7.

17. The Prophet is reported to have said: 'He is not a true Muslim who eats his fill when his next-door-neighbour is hungry.' See al-Bukhārī, *al-Adab al-Mufrad* (Cairo: Quṣayy Muḥibb al-Dīn al-Khaṭīb, A.H. 1379), p. 52.

18. See al-Ḥākim, *Al-Mustadrak 'alā aṣ-Ṣaḥīḥayn* (Aleppo, Maktab Al-Maṭbū'āt al-Islāmīyah, n.d., Vol. 2, p. 12.

19. The Prophet himself showed the way in this respect by helping a needy person to buy an axe to cut wood instead of just meeting his immediate requirements. See *Sunan Ibn Mājah, op. cit.,* Vol. 1, p. 338.

20. Qur'ān, 2: 273.

21. Qur'ān, 2: 263–4.

22. Details of this social security system are given in Chapter Two of this book.

23. For a detailed exposition of the actual working of the Islamic social security system in this period see S. M. Hasanuz Zaman, *Economic Functions of an Islamic State* (Leicester: The Islamic Foundation, 1991).

24. See 'Abd al-'Azīz Sayyid al-Ahl, *al-Khalīfah az-Zāhid 'Umar ibn 'Abd al-'Azīz,* (Beirut: Dār al-'Ilm li'l Mala'yīn, 1973), p. 222.

25. Muḥammad Ibn Sa'd, *al-Ṭabaqāt al-Kubrā* (Beirut: Dār Ṣādir li'l Ṭibā'ah wa al-Nashr, 1968), Vol. 3, p. 305.

26. For a comprehensive discussion on this subject, see Muhammad Nejatullah Siddiqi, 'The Guarantee of a Minimum Level of Living in an

Islamic State', in Munawar Iqbal (ed.), *Distributive Justice and Need Fulfilment in an Islamic Economy* (Islamabad: International Institute of Islamic Economics; Leicester: The Islamic Foundation, 1988).

27. In one of the verses of the Qur'ān it is stated, 'Hast thou observed him who belieth religion? That is he who repelleth the orphan and urgeth not the feeding of the needy' (107: 1–3). Here indifference toward the plight of the needy is equated to denial of all religion.

28. Mention of freedom from hunger and thirst and the importance of clothing and shelter is found in the Qur'ān when it is pointed out that before the descent of man on earth, God addressed Adam as follows: 'O Adam! This is an enemy unto thee and unto thy wife, so let him not drive you both out of the Garden so that thou come to toil. It is (vouchsafed) unto thee that thou hungerest not therein nor art naked, and thou thirstest not therein nor art exposed to the sun's heat' (20: 117–19).

29. See Abū Isḥāq Ibrāhim al-Shāṭibī, *al-Muwāfaqāt fī Uṣūl al-Sharī'ah* (Cairo: Maktabah al-Tijārīyah al-Kubrā, n.d.), Vol. 2, pp. 8–25.

30. '. . . We have distributed their livelihood among them in worldly life, and have raised some above others in the matter of social degrees, so that some of them may utilize the services of others in their work . . .' (43: 32).

31. Qur'ān, 26: 181.

32. Islam aims at establishing a socio-economic order where all individuals live together as members of one single family and freely help each other in time of need. It is repeatedly stated in the Qur'ān that the act of giving benefits not only the donee but the donor also as he receives God's blessing both in this world and the Hereafter. Moreover, the whole society benefits in terms of social cohesion, peace, and amity. The basic idea is that of interdependent utility functions among individuals which is a form of externality.

33. The Qur'ān states: 'Give the kinsman his due, and the needy and the wayfarer, and squander not (thy wealth) in wantonness. Lo! the squanderers were ever brothers of the devils, and the devil was ever an ingrate to his Lord' (17: 26–7).

CHAPTER 2

Policy Framework for Eradication of Poverty and Achievement of an Equitable Distribution of Income and Wealth

The Islamic teachings based on the Qur'ān and the *Sunnah* provide guidance on all aspects of human life. It is a typical feature of Islamic teachings that strictly mandatory elements are kept to a minimum while a wide area of discretion is allowed to man to organize and order his affairs. The conclusive injunctions of the Qur'ān and the *Sunnah,* from which no departure is allowed in any age, are known as *nuṣūṣ.*[1] Islam, however, allows full scope to human reasoning for finding solutions to problems on which direct guidance is not available from the Qur'ān and the *Sunnah* through a process known as *ijtihād.*[2] This chapter seeks to set out the main elements of a policy framework for eradication of poverty and achievement of an equitable distribution of income and wealth which can be discerned and deduced from Islamic teachings. The presentation is based on direct deductions from the Qur'ān and the *Sunnah* and on the writings of prominent jurists and scholars whose capacity to undertake *ijtihād* is well recognized.

Encouragement of Productive Effort

Islam takes a positive and socially interactive view of life on earth and makes no distinction between the secular and spiritual dimensions of human existence. It strongly disapproves asceticism and gives high regard to lawful economic activity. In fact, productive effort is encouraged to the point of its being a moral obligation, and the fruit of productive effort is described as a bounty from God.[3] Lack of any dichotomy between the material and spiritual sides of life invests even the material pursuits with spirituality, and it is in this sense that earning one's living through honest means is also regarded as a form of worship *('ibādah)* in Islam.

There is a good deal of discussion in juristic literature about the bearing of the notion of predestination found in some verses of the Qur'ān on man's productive endeavour. A frequently quoted verse which figures prominently in this discussion is: 'Say: Lo! my Lord enlargeth the provision for whom He will of His bondmen, and narroweth (it) for him. And whatsoever ye spend (for good) He replaceth it. And He is the best of Providers.'[4] The jurists have pointed out that verses such as these are meant to convey to man the fact of God's omnipotence and can in no way be treated as sanctioning a passive attitude toward earning one's living. Similarly, the verses which point to the fragility and transient nature of worldly wealth are meant to wean man away from an exclusive concern for amassing wealth to the neglect of his moral responsibilities rather than dampen man's honest endeavour to improve his material well being.

The work ethics of Islam can be easily discerned from the verses of the Qur'ān and the sayings of the Prophet. Man is reminded that God has caused day and night to follow each other so that man may seek his livelihood during the day and rest during the night.[5] He is encouraged to avail himself of the vast opportunities of productive enterprise afforded by the limitless bounties of God.[6] The Prophet is reported to have said: 'If God provides anyone of you with an opportunity for earning a livelihood, let him not leave it unexploited until it is exhausted or becomes disagreeable to him.'[7] He exhorted all able-bodied persons to earn their living and desist from seeking assistance from others except in the event of desperate need. He told his followers: 'A man has not earned better income than that which is from his own labour'[8] and 'The hand that spends is better than the hand that begs.'[9] The Prophet repeatedly emphasized severe religious disapprobation of the conduct of those who tend to depend on charity though they can earn enough for the fulfilment of their basic needs through their own efforts.[10]

Adoption of an Islamically-Oriented Growth Strategy

The teachings contained in the Qur'ān and the *Sunnah* provide a firm basis for achieving equitable growth to tackle the problem of poverty as also of inequalities of income and wealth. Three basic considerations, emphasized in the *sharī'ah,* provide the clues to adoption of an Islamically-oriented growth strategy which can help powerfully in realizing the Islamic vision of a just socio-economic order. These relate to the overall rate of growth, the mechanics of growth and the pattern of growth.

A number of verses in the Qur'ān point to the limitless possibilities of economic growth which man can realize in this world. The general message of Islam is for a dynamic change over time through technological advancement. The entire universe with all its natural resources has been made amenable to exploitation by man.[11] Man has been endowed with reason and intellect with which he can acquire the knowledge necessary for the utilization of natural resources for his benefit.[12] Islam sets no quantitative limits to the extent of material growth of human society but it has a lot to say about the mechanics of growth and the pattern of growth.

The mechanics of growth envisaged by Islam assigns a central role to man as vicegerent of God on earth. In keeping with man's dignified status, Islam attaches great importance to an individual's freedom in pursuing his chosen line of economic activity. Achievement of growth through regimentation is, therefore, alien to the spirit of Islam.[13]

Islam envisages productive activity to be undertaken primarily on the basis of private enterprise. Excepting certain natural resources, which should be kept under state domain in the public interest,[14] there is no restriction on individuals owning any productive asset or property. However, Islamic teachings emphasize that the right of ownership on productive assets should be so exercised that the general interests of the society are not hurt and the achievement of Islamic socio-economic objectives is facilitated. It is a fundamental doctrine of Islam that God is the real owner of all that exists, and man's ownership of any property or productive asset is in the nature of a trust.[15] Private enterprise in an Islamic system cannot, therefore, be accorded the same degree of freedom as it is supposed to enjoy in a purely *laissez-faire* system. The state, which guards the collective interests of the society, has the right to influence and regulate the working of the private sector to achieve the objectives of the Islamic system.[16]

The pattern of growth has a vital bearing on the relative welfare of different sections of the population. It has been mentioned in the first chapter that eradication of absolute poverty has the top priority in Islamic socio-economic objectives. Besides, Islamic teachings enjoin that wealth should not become 'a commodity between the rich among you'. It is obvious that some monitoring of the growth process is essential if these objectives are to be attained. Free play of market forces cannot be depended upon to generate a pattern of growth which meets the Islamic imperatives. Islam's social security system ensures that everyone has at least the minimum purchasing power to fulfil his basic needs.[17] However, to keep the financial demand on the social security system within manageable limits as also to promote general economic well-being, it is necessary that growth be broad based.

A *laissez-faire* private enterprise economy cannot guarantee that benefits of growth would be widely diffused. The working of competitive forces in such an economy may ensure 'productive efficiency' in the technical sense of the term but this can co-exist with increasing inequalities in income and wealth. A command economy, on the other hand, can cut down income inequalities through direct state action. However, the means adopted for this purpose, particularly the nationalization of means of production, are not compatible with Islamic teachings. The attainment of Islamic socio-economic objectives, therefore, calls for the adoption of an Islamically-oriented growth strategy reflecting its own values and priorities.

Generation of a maximum feasible level of employment opportunities has the strongest claim to be accorded top priority in an Islamically-oriented growth strategy. Unemployment of those who are able and willing to work is not in keeping with the status of man as the vicegerent of God on earth. Referring to several verses in the Qur'ān, the jurists have pointed out that relieving of hardship is one of the most important objectives *(maqāṣid)* of *sharī'ah.*[18] It cannot be denied that involuntary unemployment constitutes one of the worst forms of hardship. On the other hand, a high level of employment is the greatest assurance that growth would be broad based.

The teachings contained in the Qur'ān and the *Sunnah* provide only broad guidelines for economic policy formulation. It is for policy-makers in each age to devise suitable policies to attain the desired objectives in the light of these broad guidelines. Policies designed to achieve a maximum feasible level of employment would naturally differ from country to country depending on factor proportions, the state of demand, the technological choices available and other relevant factors.[19] Monetary and fiscal policies can also be made to play an especially important role in promoting employment opportunities.[20]

An Islamically-oriented growth strategy has also to concern itself with the composition of gross domestic product. It would be inconsistent with Islamic norms of justice that productive resources of the society are used for the production of luxury goods while the basic needs of the poor remain unfulfilled. The degree of state intervention in commodity markets that may be needed to ensure fulfilment of the basic needs of all would differ from case to case. Provision of public goods, which cannot be expected to be made available in sufficient measure by the market mechanism, has inevitably to be a state responsibility. Examples are education and health facilities. However, with proper motivation, voluntary effort of individuals and institutions can also be expected to contribute significantly toward the provision of such goods. Production of other goods would take place in response to market demand within the ethical constraints of an Islamic society and the requirements of social justice. Production of goods whose consumption is prohibited would not be allowed. The state may use both direct and indirect controls to the extent considered necessary to regulate the production mix of the economy to achieve the end of social justice.

Regulation of Business Practices

Islamic teachings prescribe a comprehensive code of business ethics which seeks to eliminate all exploitative practices. Business is considered a laudable activity provided it does not result in an unjust gain to any of the parties involved in a business deal. The main aim of regulating business practices is to prevent undue enrichment of some at the expense of the many and thereby to curb inequalities of income and wealth.

The general principle enunciated in the Qur'ān applicable to business dealings is that people should not devour the property of one another by wrongful means.[21] Several sayings of the Prophet give concrete expression to what is right and what is wrong in business and trade. Those who fulfil their obligations and desist from prohibited practices are promised reward in the Hereafter, and those who are neglectful are warned of punishment. Islamic teachings also envisage an active role for the state in promoting fair business practices. The Prophet, after the establishment of the Islamic state at Madinah, took steps to institutionalize arrangements for looking after the social behaviour of the people and performance of their religious duties. In the course of time, the state institution designed to promote what is proper and forbid what is improper came to be known as *ḥisbah*. The officer in charge of the *ḥisbah* was called *muḥtasib*. He was particularly entrusted with the responsibility of ensuring the observance of business ethics.[22]

Islam favours organization of production and exchange on the basis of norms provided in the *sharī'ah*. Stress is laid on the freedom of entry in all types of economic undertakings, except those reserved for the state, so that equal opportunities are available to all for productive endeavour. Monopoly as a form of business organization is greatly disfavoured. Some jurists regard it as completely forbidden while others take a more flexible approach provided the monopolist is not left wholly free to exercise his power to the detriment of public interest. Rules governing the behaviour of participants in the market are designed to ensure a just exchange. Full disclosure regarding the quantity and quality of the goods offered for sale is insisted upon. Fake publicity, adulteration, short weight, and short measurement are strictly forbidden.

Islamic teachings strongly deprecate all practices which interfere with normal supply of goods to the market, resulting in an artificial increase in prices, an unjust loss to the consumer and an unjust gain to the businessman. The Prophet specifically expressed his disapproval of the conduct of those intermediaries who disrupted the flow of village products to the city markets to make a gain for themselves which entailed a loss both to the producers and the consumers. Hoarding of goods and cornering of stocks, particularly of foodstuffs, with a view to benefiting from the resultant rise in prices is considered a great sin in Islam.

The jurists have worked hard to scrutinize various types of sale and purchase transactions in the light of the sayings of the Prophet to determine their permissibility or otherwise in an Islamic society. All transactions in which the commodity offered for sale either does not exist or is not well determined lack validity.[23] Enhancement of the price of a merchandise by fictitious tender of a high price is prohibited. These and other prescriptions found in the law books of Islam are meant to promote fair business practices and prevent undue enrichment of a particular class of society at the expense of others.

Equality of Opportunity

Equality in basic economic rights is one of the fundamental principles of Islam. One of these basic rights is that every individual should have an opportunity to develop his inborn faculties to the fullest extent possible and choose a profession according to his aptitude. It is in recognition of this principle that a competitive market structure, which assures freedom of entry to all, is the one favoured by Islam. Access to natural resources also has to be free of any sort of discrimination. Islam is also strongly opposed to social stratification. Where stratification is present, privileges tend to remain with the elite groups. A number of opportunities are not open to the larger strata of the population; this perpetuates inequalities of income and wealth. Islam's commitment to social justice underlines the heavy emphasis on equality of opportunity.

Equal access to educational facilities is one of the key factors in promoting equality of opportunity. Universal education breaks up social stratification and prevents the development of labour market segmentation, thereby restraining the growth in income inequalities. Islam exhorts its followers to acquire knowledge.[24] It is the responsibility of the state to so devise the educational programmes that all sections of the population derive adequate benefit from them. Unless sufficient care is taken, the benefits of the educational programmes may flow disproportionately toward higher income groups. This may serve to increase rather than decrease income inequalities. It is only by careful planning that educational programmes can serve as an instrument promoting both growth and equality.

Besides education, there are a number of ways in which the state can promote equality of opportunity. The way in which the banking and financial system of a country operates has an important bearing on the pattern of income distribution. If the banking system extends financial facilities only to the rich and propertied classes, it may lead to further enrichment of these classes and accentuation of inequalities of income and wealth. On the other hand, widespread access to financial facilities from the banks can help greatly in improving the income status of poorer sections of the population. Government controls and regulations affecting various types of productive activity, investment and imports also have a bearing on the pattern of income distribution. The forms these policy interventions take affect different classes of the population differently. The distributive effects of alternative policy options have, therefore, to be kept in view in deciding upon a particular course of action.

Property Rights and Obligations in Islam

Property rights in Islam are governed by the basic principle that the real ownership of everything belongs to God. Man's ownership of any property is, therefore, in the nature of a trust and is subject to the terms of that trust. The terms of this trust can be ascertained from the guidance available in the Qur'ān and the *Sunnah*. From the actions of the Prophet it is easily discerned that he classified property in two broad categories. One consists of certain kinds of natural wealth which are excluded from the scope of private ownership. Four such resources specifically mentioned by the Prophet are water, herbage, fire, and salt.[25] The jurists are generally agreed that other natural resources having similar properties can be added to the list.[26] The second category consists of all those items which are not held as a common trust and in which private property rights are recognized.

Property rights in Islam carry certain legal obligations. The first requirement is that property should have been acquired through Islamically permissible means. The Qur'ān cautions: 'Devour not the property of any one of you wrongfully . . .'[27] Another requirement is that it should be put to proper use. Wasteful use of one's property is disapproved.[28] Leaving the production resources unutilized is also disapproved.[29] Use of one's property in a manner which damages the interests of others is disallowed.[30] The obligation attaching to property ownership which has the greatest bearing on the distribution of income and wealth relates to sharing of one's wealth with the poorer sections of the society. The Qur'ān declares that 'the poor have a right in the wealth of the rich'.[31] This sharing takes many forms. There is a compulsory contribution, known as *zakāh,* which all property owners are required to make for the uplift of the poor in accordance with set rules and regulations.[32] It is the responsibility of the state to make arrangements for the collection and disbursement of *zakāh*. Besides this compulsory levy, which helps solve the problem of poverty in a generalized manner through the agency of the state, Islam places particular responsibility on all well-to-do members of the society to help their close relatives through an institutional mechanism known as *nafaqāt* (obligatory maintenance by relatives), which can be given legislative effect if found necessary.[33]

There is another dimension to the question of property

rights which has a bearing on the distribution of income and wealth. This relates to the degree of social control on private ownership rights and the circumstances justifying abrogation or abridgement of such rights. Islam, as mentioned earlier, does not aim at obliterating all inequalities of income and wealth. There is nothing objectionable in certain individuals obtaining and retaining title to a larger amount of property and assets provided these have been acquired lawfully and obligations attaching to such property ownership have been duly discharged. The jurists are of the view that in ordinary circumstances private property rights are to be treated as inviolable. However, in compelling circumstances, individual ownership of particular kinds of property or productive assets can be subjected to certain limits in the larger public interest. Expropriation of lawfully acquired property without paying any compensation is strictly disallowed. Fair compensation is to be paid by the state to property holders whenever it is decided to take over any kind of property beyond a set limit to serve a social purpose.[34]

Inheritance Laws

Islamic inheritance laws are aimed at achieving a wide distribution of wealth among the relatives of the deceased. The inheritors include the members of the inner family – the children, parents, and spouse – but other relatives also find a place in the scheme of distribution. The basis of the distribution is given in the following verses of the Qur'ān:

> Allah chargeth you concerning (the provisions for) your children: to the male the equivalent of the portion of two females, and if there be women more than two, then theirs is two-thirds of the inheritance, and if there be one (only), then the half. And to his parents a sixth of the inheritance if he have a son; and if he have no son and his parents are his heirs, then to his mother appertaineth the third; and if he have brethren, then to his mother appertaineth the sixth, after any legacy he may have bequeathed, or debt (hath been paid). Your parents or your children: Ye know not which of them

is nearer unto you in usefulness. It is an injunction from Allah. Lo! Allah is Knower, Wise.

And unto you belongeth a half of that which your wives leave, if they have no child; but if they have a child then unto you the fourth of that which they leave, after any legacy they may have bequeathed, or debt (they may have contracted, hath been paid). And unto them belongeth the fourth of that which you leave if ye have no child, but if ye have a child then the eighth of that which ye leave, after any legacy ye may have bequeathed, or debt (ye may have contracted, hath been paid). And if a man or a woman have a distant heir (having left neither parent nor child), and he (or she) have a brother or a sister (only on the mother's side then to each of them twain the brother and the sister) the sixth, and if they be more than two, then they shall be sharers in the third, after any legacy that may have been bequeathed or debt (contracted) not injuring (the heirs by willing away more than a third of the heritage) hath been paid. A commandment from Allah. Allah is Knower, Indulgent. (4: 11–12)

They ask thee for a pronouncement. Say: Allah hath pronounced for you concerning distant kindred. If a man dies childless and he have a sister, hers is half the heritage, and he would have inherited from her had she died childless. And if there be two sisters, then theirs are two-thirds of the heritage, and if there be brethren, men and women, unto the male is the equivalent of the share of two females. Allah expoundeth unto you, so that ye err not. Allah is Knower of all things. (4: 176)

The jurists have, on the basis of the regulations laid down in the Qur'ān and the sayings of the Prophet, evolved elaborate tables to show how the estate of the deceased is to be distributed. The main features of the Islamic inheritance laws can be summarized as follows:

a. A testator may make bequests to the extent of a maximum of one third of his or her property remaining after payment of all debts. Out of the rest, or if he dies intestate, out of the balance left after the payment of all debts, the inheritors receive their due shares.

b. A long list of inheritors has been prescribed and their shares fixed to effect a wide dispersal of the estate left by the deceased.

c. Women are also entitled to a share in inheritance along with men. The share of women, in most cases, is half that of male heirs in the same category. The higher share of men is on account of the responsibilities they carry for the maintenance of the family.

d. Among the same category of heirs is absolute uniformity of treatment. No distinction has been made among children on the basis of precedence in birth, and an equal share accrues to the elder and the younger.

In order to ensure that the inheritance laws serve their intended purpose, the property holders have been denied any right to deprive a legal heir of his or her share or to make any modification in the prescribed share of any heir. It is also forbidden to make a bequest in favour of a heir. Thus, no heir can receive anything from the estate of the deceased over and above his or her own share of the inheritance. The Qur'ān also advises the inheritors to give away a part of their inherited wealth, which they obtain without putting in their own labour, to such needy relatives as are not entitled to any share in the distribution of the deceased's estate as well as to orphans and other needy persons at the time of the division of the shares.[35] Considering the long chain of beneficiaries and the mandatory nature of the detailed instructions, the Islamic inheritance laws play an important role in reducing inequalities of income and wealth from generation to generation.

Factor Shares and Functional Distribution of Income

Islamic teachings have an important bearing on factor shares and functional distribution of income which in turn have implications for size distribution of personal income. Islam employs a distinctive approach in identifying factors of production and regulating the return on these factors. A sharp distinction is made between money capital and real capital. Money capital is denied entitlement to any return whatsoever if it is just lent to someone for a specified period of time. This means that no one can earn any income in an Islamic economy by charging interest. Money capital can, however, be provided to others for being invested in any productive undertaking on the basis of profit sharing. Money capital can also be converted into real capital through acquisition of durable goods which can be leased on rent. Land is recognized as a factor of production, and its ownership can provide a legitimate source of earning in ways approved by the *sharī'ah*. Labour, as a factor of production, is accorded a dignity in keeping with man's status as vicegerent of God on earth. The return on labour can take the form of wages or a share in the profit of enterprise where it combines with another factor of production in a productive process.

The giving and taking of interest is strictly prohibited in Islam. Abstinence from interest is enjoined by the verses in the Qur'ān[36] as well as the sayings of the Prophet. The jurists and other scholars have written extensively on the rationale behind the prohibition of interest. It has been pointed out that interest charged on loans taken for meeting essential consumption requirements amounts to taking advantage of a man's weak economic position and is repugnant to the spirit of Islam whose underlying philosophy is one of *al-'adl wa'l-iḥsān* (justice and benevolence). Interest on loans taken for production purposes is also considered an inequitable transaction. The inequity arises from the fact that the borrower is obliged to pay interest even though he may have incurred a loss. Even when a profit is made, the fixed rate of interest can prove an onerous burden if the rate of profit earned is less than the rate of interest payable. When money is invested in a productive undertaking, the actual outcome in terms of profit or loss is not certain. To insist on a 'pound of flesh' irrespective of the economic circumstances of the borrower of money militates against the Islamic norm of justice.

While any return on capital in the form of interest is prohibited in Islam, there is no objection to getting a return on capital under profit/loss sharing arrangements approved by *sharī'ah.* The fundamental features of profit/loss sharing arrangements which are in tune with the ethos of the value system of Islam are available in juristic literature. The two forms of such an arrangement which have been extensively discussed are known as *muḍārabah* (or *qirāḍ* or *muqāraḍah*) and *mushārakah.* In *muḍārabah,* one party provides the necessary money capital, and the other supplies the human capital needed for carrying on a productive activity. When capital is provided entirely by one party and enterprise or labour entirely by another party, the profit earned can be divided between the parties in proportions agreed upon and stipulated in the agreement. However, in the event of a loss, the entire loss has to be borne by the provider of capital unless it is due to the negligence of the worker or the entrepreneur. If there is more than one provider of capital, profit can be distributed among them in agreed proportions, while loss is to be shared by them strictly in proportion to their respective capital contributions. In the other form of a participative arrangement known as *mushārakah,* all the parties contribute to the capital employed and they also participate in managing the enterprise, though not necessarily equally. Profit is shared in pre-agreed proportions but the loss, if any, is borne strictly in proportion to the capital contributed by each party.

The requirement, both under *muḍārabah* and *mushārakah* that loss has to be shared strictly in proportion to the capital contribution while profits can be shared in any pre-agreed proportions, is meant to ensure equity while providing sufficient flexibility in working out business-finance relationships. The basis of cooperation between capital and enterprise in Islam is the sharing of risks and gains between them. In the event of a loss under a *muḍārabah* or *mushārakah* agreement, the providers of capital suffer an erosion in the amount of capital invested while the party or parties contributing enterprise suffer in the form of not getting any reward for their effort. The loss, in other words, falls on the respective 'contribution' of the factors of production. In a profit situation, however, the shares in profit distribution need not be strictly in proportion to the capital invested as providers of capital may participate in the management of business in varying degrees and may therefore deserve differential treatment.

It will be seen from the foregoing that the Islamic system does not permit an addition to the wealth of the owners of money capital until the use of this capital results in the creation of additional wealth. The possibility of additional wealth flowing to the owners of money capital from loss-incurring enterprises is obviated. In a profit situation, the proportion in which profit is shared between the providers of capital and users of capital will generally be determined through the market forces influencing the demand for and supply of capital. The technique of *muḍārabah* has the potential of considerably improving the financial position of low income groups by widening the choice available to them to set up their own business rather than be confined to wage-earning occupations. The overall outcome of these arrangements is likely to be beneficial for the pattern of income distribution.

It is necessary to revert here once again to the basic difference between interest and profit, and the reasons why Islam prohibits interest but regards profit as a legitimate return on capital and entrepreneurial effort. A return on money lent in the form of interest, even when borrowing is for productive purposes, is prohibited because it is pre-determined to be positive irrespective of the ultimate outcome of business, which may be positive or negative depending on a whole host of factors, some of which are beyond the control of the entrepreneur who borrows the capital. On the other hand, the earning of profit is uncertain and its actual quantum, positive or negative, depends on the operating results of the business concern. Payment of something definite in return for something uncertain militates against the Islamic concept of justice and equity while an uncertain return on productive activity whose outcome is uncertain is fully in harmony with it. However, Islamic teachings seek to limit profit earnings also within reasonable bounds in the interest of an equitable distribution of income and wealth.

The emphasis on free entry in the market, preservation of competitive market conditions, and the institution of *ḥisbah* to oversee business practices are all intended to safeguard against the emergence of undue profits.

While there is a consensus among jurists on the illegitimacy of interest and permissibility of profit, there has been some difference of views on the question of land rent. The right of the owner to cultivate his own land and appropriate the accruing surplus over cost is not disputed. Controversy centres around giving the land to another person on rent or on the basis of share cropping. Some jurists have held giving of land on rent to be against *sharī'ah*. This opinion is based on certain sayings of the Prophet. It is reported, for example, that the Prophet said: 'It is better for you to give your land to your brother rather than charge from him a fixed produce for it.' The practice of renting land to a cultivator in return for a fixed percentage of crops plus a fixed quantity grown in certain fixed areas of that piece of land, prevalent at that time, was also reportedly disapproved by the Prophet. Other jurists have pointed out that these and certain other sayings of the Prophet should not be interpreted to mean that the Prophet had completely outlawed the renting of land. They have cited other sayings of the Prophet which allow renting of land. A large number of scholars are of the view that the prohibition relates only to the renting of land in return for a fixed amount of produce and reservation of produce of some particular portion of the land for the landlord, while renting of land in terms of a fixed amount of money is permissible.[37]

Questions have been raised as to how a fixed rent on land can be justified when Islam strictly prohibits a fixed return on money capital. The jurists have resolved this issue by pin-pointing the difference between the nature of money capital and that of real capital. Money is a commodity from which one cannot derive any benefit until something is bought with this money. Besides, money is not subject to physical depreciation. Money capital is therefore not entitled to any return when it is just transferred from one hand to another by way of a loan. Items of real capital, including land, on the other hand, are directly usable and suffer physical depreciation when use is made of them. Charging of fixed rent on such items is therefore not unlawful. The jurists have also opined that charging of rent on items of real capital is justifiable only if they are in a readily usable form. Rent cannot be charged if the usability of an item is in doubt. Barren land, for example, on which no cultivation is possible cannot be given out on rent for agricultural purposes.

The permissibility or otherwise of *muzāra'ah* (share cropping) has been the subject matter of intense debate among jurists. Both those favouring it and those opposed to it have cited sayings of the Prophet to support their viewpoint.[38] A majority of the jurists have held share cropping to be permissible on the basis of the argument that the Prophet had only prohibited those forms of share cropping where one party made it a condition that he will get a specific quantity of produce or that the product of some particular part of land will go to him.

The jurists have recognized that conditions may arise when one party may seek to extract undue advantage in fixing the land rent or his share in agricultural produce in share cropping by virtue of a stronger bargaining position. They favour state intervention in such cases to safeguard the interest of the weaker party.

Islam is strongly opposed to exploitation of labour and seeks to promote the greatest amity between employers and employees. The Qur'ān urges people to 'withhold not things justly due to others'.[39] The Prophet held workers in high esteem.[40] The aim of Islam is to generate a proper working relationship between the employers and the employees which safeguards the dignity of the employee as a human being and also does not harm the interests of the employers. Islam's emphasis on the preservation of human dignity of all citizens cannot allow wages to be determined exclusively by the free play of market forces which, in conditions of abundant supply of labour, might push wages even below the subsistence level. Several sayings of the Prophet emphasize that people who take work from others should ensure that at least the basic needs of the latter are met.[41] The concept of a 'just' wage in Islam is, therefore, not related to the marginal productivity of the worker but to the cost of living. Since the state is ultimately responsible for the welfare of each and every citizen, it can resort to statutory fixing of minimum wages to ensure receipt of a just wage by the workers. The state is also expected to ensure congenial working conditions for the employees.[42]

Encouragement of Voluntary Spending for the Welfare of the Poor

According to Islamic teachings, it is obligatory on all persons of means to spend a part of their wealth for the welfare of the poor and the needy. The Qur'ān enjoins such spending without expecting any return or reward in this world and for the sheer purpose of earning God's pleasure and benediction in the Hereafter. The Qur'ān also enjoins that such spending should not cause any embarrassment to those being helped and should not be accompanied by any reminders to the recipients.[43] The obligation to help the poor and the needy is based on the premise that God alone is the Creator and real Owner of all wealth, and what a man gets in this world from his efforts is His Grace. Spending a part of his wealth on the poor and the needy is thus an expression of man's gratitude to God. It is God's munificence that He regards the amount thus spent as a 'goodly loan' which in recompense is increased manifold.[44]

The most frequently recurring terms in the Qur'ān in the context of spending for the welfare of the poor and the needy are *infāq* (voluntary spending), *iḥsān* (benevolence), *zakāh* (poor due), *ṣadaqah* (charity), and *iṭ'ām* (feeding). Among these, *zakāh* represents a fixed and mandatory payment;[45] the others stand for voluntary help and payments. Feeding the hungry is stressed again and again so much so that repelling the orphan and neglect of the feeding of the destitute are equated to denial of the religion itself.[46] The amount of wealth that should be spent in the way of God, after the obligation to pay *zakāh* has been discharged, has not been specified in precise quantitative terms. However, there is a general indication in one of the verses in the Qur'ān that any surplus above one's genuine needs should be so spent.[47] The Arabic word used is *al-'afw* which has been translated by various scholars as 'beyond your needs', 'superfluous', 'left over', 'left after meeting your needs', and so on. This verse has been interpreted by some to mean that one should give away in charity everything one earns beyond what one needs for meeting the immediate requirements of oneself and one's family.[48] The consensus of jurists has, however, always been that Islam does not disallow saving, and the intent of the verse is to dissuade people from extravagance and to provide an incentive for them to excel each other in spending for the welfare of the poor and the needy.

Islam emphasizes voluntary spending for the welfare of the poor and the needy not only to banish poverty but also to promote social cohesion and harmony. A verse in the Qur'ān cautions that lack of such spending can lead to a society's ruination.[49] The implication is that if people are self-centred and oblivious of the hardships of the poorer sections of the society, they can all come to grief because of absence of fellow feeling. History shows that callousness toward the plight of the poor results eventually in social disruption, discord and civil commotion. On the other hand, if people practice *infāq* and derive satisfaction from helping the poor and the needy, society as a whole gains in terms of peace and amity.[50]

The Islamic system incorporates several institutional devices to foster voluntary spending for the welfare of the poor. One of these is known as *waqf.* This essentially implies setting aside certain assets, like land and buildings, for exclusive use for specific purposes under a legal deed. The *waqf* so established can no longer be sold or otherwise dispensed with, but the person establishing the *waqf* can designate the nature of the disbursements to be made out of the income of the property. The *waqf* is a useful institutional device for transferring wealth from private ownership to collective ownership for socially beneficial purposes. Its use dates from before the time of the Prophet.[51]

Another institutional device to help the poor is known as *manīḥah.* This involves granting of usufruct of a productive asset to a needy person free of charge for a specific period. This was one of the devices introduced by the Prophet to enable the residents of Madinah to extend help to the first immigrants to this city state established by him on his migration from Makkah. Six kinds of *manīḥah* have been reported specifically in the sayings of the Prophet. These are: *manīḥah* of dirhams (money), riding animals, milk animals, agricultural lands, fruit-bearing trees and houses.[52]

Fiscal and Monetary Policies

Fiscal and monetary policies are expected to play a very important role in eradicating poverty and keeping inequalities of income and wealth within acceptable limits in an Islamic economy. The Qur'ān and the *Sunnah* do not prescribe any rigid system of public finance. The major emphasis is on the state's responsibility to come to the rescue of the needy, and in this context collection and distribution of *zakāh* on the part of the state has been made obligatory.[53] The fiscal system in the early Islamic period was very simple[54] but the succeeding generations have been free to devise a system suited to their needs keeping in view the Islamic imperatives of justice and equity and keeping away from practices which are prohibited.

Islamic teachings do not bind the state with regard to particular tax measures that may be adopted to achieve the various fiscal policy objectives. However, they do emphasize that taxes should be imposed only to finance 'essential expenditure' and the tax burden should be equitably distributed.[55] Taxes cannot make the poor richer but they should at least not aggravate inequalities of income and wealth. In the early Islamic period, taxes were mostly levied on certain types of assets and income accruing from specific assets but there is nothing in Islamic teachings to prevent the state from levying taxes on some other base, such as income in general, or expenditure or sales.

The Islamic approach to eradication of poverty and reduction in inequalities of income and wealth is not merely redistributive. As mentioned earlier, Islam seeks to tackle the problem of poverty through, among other things, the encouragement of productive effort and generation of maximum feasible employment opportunities. The taxation policies have, therefore, to be so devised as to encourage investment, preserve incentives for work effort and bring about such changes in relative prices in factor and commodity markets as favour increased employment opportunities. In this context, advantage can be taken of the latest research in the field of optimal taxation to evolve tax policies best suited to raise a given revenue in such a way as to minimize the welfare loss, subject to socially determined distributional weights.

As for public expenditure policies, jurists are agreed that (a) removal of hardship and injury must take precedence over the provision of comforts and (b) the larger interest of the majority should take precedence over the narrower interest of a minority.[56] Eradication of poverty and removal of the hardships of the poorer sections of the population figure prominently in the priorities of public expenditure in an Islamic economy. The state must ensure that sufficient resources are earmarked in the public expenditure programme to effectively tackle the problem of poverty and to satisfy the basic needs of all citizens.[57] The amount of resources needed for the purpose would depend on the number of people below the poverty line and the extent of the poverty gap. According to Islamic teachings, the first recourse in securing the needed resources would be from the proceeds obtained from *zakāh.* If these prove insufficient, the deficiency would be met from other budgetary resources.

Provision of such public goods as improve the living conditions of poorer sections of society and facilitate the realization of their full productive potential will also figure prominently in an Islamically-oriented public expenditure programme. This will involve greater emphasis on projects which upgrade health, education, and housing facilities for the poor. Provision of subsidies, if any, in the budget of an Islamic economy would only be justified if it brings a net increase in the general welfare of the poorer sections of the society.

Monetary policy in an Islamic economy is also expected to contribute significantly to eradication of poverty and reduction in inequalities of income and wealth. In the context of Islamic teachings, this would specifically require (a) discouragement of extravagant spending and wasteful use of resources, (b) curbing of speculative transactions, (c) promotion of employment, and (d) regulation of the use of the financial resources of the banking system to help achieve the growth and egalitarian objectives of an Islamic economy. Monetary policy in an Islamic economy cannot afford to be value-neutral. It cannot allow unrestricted use of the financial resources of the banking system primarily with reference to the criterion of 'creditworthiness' as this may lead to an ever widening gulf between the rich and the poor and a pattern of resource allocation which is sub-optimal from the viewpoint of an Islamically-oriented growth strategy. Monetary policy would need to be consciously directed to so regulate the use of the financial resources of the banking system that it helps significantly in reducing inequalities of income and wealth and achieving a product mix that is in line with Islamic priorities.

Access to financial facilities available from banks is an important determinant of one's capacity to take advantage of profitable avenues of productive endeavour. The poorer sections of society such as the unemployed and those engaged in low productivity occupations can be helped to improve their economic position if banks extend financial assistance to them for sound business propositions. However, banks most often do not provide financial assistance to 'micro-entrepreneurs' because they do not possess sufficient security to pledge with them to satisfy their criteria of creditworthiness.[58] Popularization of Islamic financing techniques like *muḍārabah* which emphasize the profit potential of a concern rather than its ability to pledge acceptable security provides an economically efficient way of using the banking system to achieve the egalitarian aims of an Islamic society.[59] Monetary policy can help in this respect by using moral suasion as well as by specifying the proportion of total financial assistance that has to be compulsorily disbursed by individual banks in the form of *muḍārabah* finance to people of small means.

Fiscal and monetary policies in an Islamic economy are also expected to promote monetary stability which, among other things, safeguards the interests of the poor. The Qur'ān exhorts: 'Give just measure and weight nor withhold from the people the things that are their due.'[60] Inflation militates against the Islamic ideal of giving fair measure of value in all transactions. Deflation is often associated with growing unemployment. Both inflation and deflation impose a welfare cost on the society and cause severest hardship to the poorest sections of the population. Pursuit of appropriate monetary and fiscal policies which safeguard monetary stability and promote a high level of employment is, therefore, of prime importance in the context of the Islamic stress on justice and equity.

Islam's Social Security System

Islamic teachings assign to the state the ultimate responsibility of ensuring at least a basic minimum standard of living for all citizens. Primarily it is one's own duty to earn a livelihood to meet one's needs and those of one's family. However, in case one is either unable to earn a livelihood or one's earnings do not suffice to meet one's basic needs, one becomes entitled to social support. Islamic teachings make it morally incumbent on the rich to help the poor and promise great reward in the Hereafter to those who spend liberally for the welfare of the needy. People are exhorted to show special consideration to the needs of poor relatives.[61] The family laws of Islam give legal right to certain close relatives to claim maintenance support from those in a position to help.[62] The state is expected to motivate the people to discharge their responsibility in respect of help to the poor and the needy. At the same time, it is incumbent on the state to establish a social security system under its own auspices in which the religiously ordained levy of *zakāh* plays a central role.[63]

Islam's concern for the poor is evident from the verses in the Qur'ān which were revealed to the Prophet even before the first Islamic state took shape in Madinah. The believers were urged to feed the hungry and also to keep reminding each other to help the poor and the needy. In one of the verses, repelling the orphan and neglect of the feeding of the destitute are equated to denial of the religion itself.[64]

People were told that the poor had a right in the wealth of the rich.[65] The term *zakāh*[66] was used to define that portion of a man's wealth which was designated for the poor to seek God's pleasure. Those who did not spend a part of their wealth for the welfare of the poor were warned of severest chastisement in the Hereafter. However, no detailed regulations for the payment of *zakāh* were laid down, and discharging of this responsibility rested with the individual himself. It was after the establishment of the Islamic state in Madinah that *zakāh* took the form of a state levy. In one of the verses of the Qur'ān, the Prophet was instructed: 'Take alms of their wealth, wherewith thou mayst purify them and mayst make them grow . . .'[67] This was deemed a clear-cut assignment to the state to organize a system of collection and disbursement of *zakāh*.

It is pertinent to mention here that though *zakāh* was made a state levy, this did not detract from its religious character. The Qur'ān continued to remind the believers that faithful payment of the *zakāh* is one of the essential attributes of a Muslim. Denial of the obligation to pay *zakāh* places one outside the fold of Islam, and one who refrains from paying it without denying its obligation is guilty of committing a sin which is severely punishable in the Hereafter.

Zakāh is a state levy whose proceeds are earmarked for specific purposes. These have been laid down in the Qur'ān as follows: 'The alms are only for the poor and the needy, and those who collect them, and those whose hearts are to be reconciled, and to free the captives and the debtors, and for the cause of Allah and (for) the wayfarers: a duty imposed by Allah. Allah is Knower, Wise.'[68] There is general agreement that the first priority in the use of *zakāh* funds has to be accorded to the alleviation of poverty through assistance to the poor and the needy. The jurists differ with regard to the line of distinction between the poor *(fuqarā')* and the needy *(masākīn)*. According to some jurists the *fuqarā'* are those who are deserving of help but do not go out to seek help while *masākīn* are those who seek help. According to some other jurists, *fuqarā'* are those who are in utter destitution while *masākīn* are those who have some resources but not enough to meet all their basic needs.

The manner in which the proceeds of *zakāh* should be used to help the poor and the needy has been discussed extensively in juristic literature.[69] It has been emphasized that *zakāh* proceeds should be disbursed in such a way that the self-respect of the recipients is not hurt. Those who are unable to work, say, due to physical disability, old age, or illness should be provided with sufficient resources to relieve their hardship. The incomes of those who are not able to earn enough for assuring a basic minimum standard of living for themselves and their dependent family members should be supplemented by transfers in cash or kind. However, maximum effort should be exerted to use the proceeds of *zakāh* in such a manner that recipients become self-supporting in the course of time.

The proceeds of *zakāh* can be used for provision of public goods provided these are exclusively for the benefit of the poor and the needy. Since it is difficult in practice to maintain such exclusiveness, the jurists generally favour the use of general funds of the treasury for such purposes.

While the Qur'ān specified the uses of *zakāh,* it did not lay down the specific characteristics of the levy such as its extent and scope, the items on which it is to be paid, and the rate of levy on different items. These were prescribed by the Prophet, and are to be found in his reported instructions on the subject. Over time a vast literature has grown up on various juristic issues related to *zakāh*. Though the jurists differ on certain matters, there is broad agreement on most of the fundamental aspects of the levy.

It is fully agreed that because of its explicit religious character, *zakāh* is to be collected by the state from Muslims only. It is not necessary that the state should collect the entire amount of *zakāh* due from a person. To the extent that the full *zakāh* due from a person is not collected by the state, the individual responsibility for disbursing *zakāh* for the persons specified in the Qur'ān remains in effect.

In the early Islamic period, *zakāh* was payable on gold, silver, merchandise, livestock, treasure trove, and mineral and agricultural produce. Applying one of the methodologies of *ijtihād* known as *qiyās* (analogical deduction), the jurists are agreed that in modern times *zakāh* is also to be paid on holdings of currency and various types of financial assets like bank deposits, shares and securities. Items in personal use, and specifically the following are not subject to *zakāh*: the house used by the owner for his own residence and of his family, wearing apparel, household utensils, animals or any other means of transportation in personal use, and articles of adornment if not made of gold and silver. There is a difference of opinion on whether fixed assets are also subject to *zakāh*. Agricultural land is unanimously held to be outside the purview of *zakāh*. On the same analogy, many jurists regard other fixed assets like factory buildings, machinery, plant and equipment as not being subject to *zakāh*. Some jurists, however, are of the view that such fixed assets should be liable for payment of *zakāh*. It has also been suggested that earnings from rented land and buildings should be treated akin to agricultural produce for the levy of *zakāh*. Some jurists favour the imposition of *zakāh* on wages and salaries as these are received, while others are of the opinion that the base for *zakāh* should be the annual salary net of deductions of debts and living expenses.[70]

The *niṣāb* (the minimum quantity or amount of an asset which makes it liable to *zakāh*) for different items was prescribed by the Prophet; and there is *ijmā‘* (consensus of jurists) that no variation from the instructions in this respect is permissible. The *niṣāb* for gold is 20 dinārs or 85 grams while for silver it is 200 dirhams or 595 grams. The *niṣāb* for cash, other financial assets and merchandise is similar to that for gold and silver. In the early Islamic period, 20 dinārs were equivalent in value to 200 dirhams. Over time, silver has become cheaper relative to gold. There is a difference of opinion among the jurists whether the minimum holding at which cash, other financial assets, and merchandise should be considered liable to payment of *zakāh* should be equivalent to 20 dinārs of gold or 200 dirhams of silver. Some jurists favour equivalence in terms of dirhams as this would serve to enlarge the receipts from *zakāh* and would be beneficial to the poor. Others favour equivalence in terms of dinārs because of the general rise in the cost of living compared to the early Islamic period. The *niṣāb* for agricultural produce is 5 *wasq* or 950 kg. in the case of produce measured by capacity and equivalent value of staple grain in other cases. The *niṣāb* in the case of livestock differs by type of animal. It is 5 in number in the case of camels, 30 in the case of bovine animals, and 40 in the case of sheep and goats. There is no *niṣāb* in the case of treasure trove. The position in regard to *niṣāb* on mineral produce in the early Islamic period is not known with certainty. According to some jurists, there is no stipulation with regard to minimum holding in the case of mineral produce while others consider it subject to levy if the value of the quantity produced in a year is commensurate to that prescribed for merchandise.

The rates of *zakāh* on various items were also prescribed by the Prophet, and these also are regarded as invariant. The lowest rate of 2.5 per cent is applicable in the case of gold, silver, cash, other financial assets and merchandise. In the case of agricultural produce, the rate is 10 per cent for crops irrigated by rainfall and 5 per cent for crops grown on land which is artificially irrigated. The rates of *zakāh* applicable to the various categories of livestock are based on a detailed schedule as laid down by the Prophet.[71] The rate is 20 per cent in the case of treasure trove. As for minerals, the position in the early Islamic period is not known with certainty. Some jurists regard mineral produce subject to *zakāh* at 2.5 per cent while others are of the view that it is subject to *khums,* that is, a levy of 20 per cent.

The liability for the payment of *zakāh* arises consequent to assets equal to more than the *niṣāb* having been in the ownership and possession of someone for one full year.[72] This condition attaches to most assets subject to *zakāh* but does not apply in the case of agricultural produce. *Zakāh* is payable only once in respect of the same asset in a *zakāh* year but *zakāh* on agricultural produce, also known as *'ushr,* is payable on the harvesting of each crop.

There have at times been suggestions that to increase the potential yield from *zakāh,* the rates of *zakāh* on various items should not be considered immutable. However, such views have found very little support in the Muslim world. The general consensus remains that any variation in the rates or *niṣāb* of *zakāh* would seriously compromise the sanctity of *zakāh* which is regarded as a form of *'ibādah* (worship) in Islam, and could open the door for changes which may introduce erratic and arbitrary elements in a stable institution. It has also been pointed out that *zakāh* even with invariant *niṣāb* and invariant rates has the potential of mobilizing substantial resources for alleviation of poverty because the *niṣāb* is low and the base of the levy is fairly wide. In fact, the base is so wide that almost everyone except the very poor has to pay something by way of *zakāh*. In certain country studies, *zakāh* has been found to have the potential of transferring 3–4 per cent of gross domestic product every year to poorer sections of the population.[73] The position would, of course, vary from country to country depending on the pattern of its income distribution and its structural characteristics.

Zakāh is the cornerstone of Islam's social security system. The bulk of the financing needed for assuring at least a basic minimum standard of living for all citizens, which is the objective of the system, is expected to come from *zakāh* proceeds. However, in case proceeds from *zakāh* do not suffice for the purpose, these have to be supplemented from the general budgetary resources to the extent considered necessary. A basic principle of public finance in Islam is that whereas the proceeds from *zakāh* cannot be spent for purposes other than those specified in the Qur'ān, there is no restriction on the transfer of resources from the general budget to the welfare budget for the augmentation of the social security fund.[74] The Prophet is reported to have said: 'And in your wealth are also obligations beyond *zakāh*.'[75] How much of the general budgetary resources should be transferred to the welfare budget is a question that would obviously need to be decided keeping in view the other pressing demands on the state's budgetary resources. It would in any case be essential that a pragmatic view is taken of the standard of need fulfilment keeping in view the general economic conditions of the country so that the state is able to fulfil its other responsibilities along with its responsibility of assuring at least a basic minimum standard of living for all its citizens.

Islam's social security system is meant to be a highly personalized system in which individual needs are addressed in accordance with the nature and intensity of these needs. In certain sayings of the Prophet the head of the state is likened to the head of a family, and made responsible for the welfare of each and every citizen.[76] Just as the head of a family assists the members of his family in accordance with their individual needs and requirements consistent with the resources available to him, the state is expected to ascertain the unfulfilled basic needs of its citizens and do the best it can to fulfil these needs. State assistance to the poor and the needy can take multifarious forms. In the case of those unable to work due to physical disability, the state is expected to provide enough to meet their basic needs. Uncared for orphans and widows are also eligible for similar assistance. In the case of able-bodied men, Islam's social security system is expected to help them in earning their own living. To achieve this purpose, state assistance can take the form of the provision of small amounts of capital funds to enable them to set up their own micro-enterprises. State assistance can also take the form of defraying the cost of such training as will enable them to acquire certain skills which in turn may enable them to become self supporting. Children belonging to poor families can be provided with scholarships and stipends to pursue their education. Distress relief also falls within the jurisdiction of Islam's social security system. The earning members of the society are expected to live within their means. However, those whose earnings do not suffice to meet their basic needs can be provided with an income supplement. Wide discretion is allowed to the authorities responsible for the proper administration of the social security system to meet other genuine requirements of the poor and the needy. Thus, funds can be provided for meeting marriage expenses in really hard cases and for paying off the debt of persons in a destitute condition.

Islam's social security system is organized on a state-wide basis but it also has a pronounced local character. The poor of a certain locality are accorded the first claim on the *zakāh* collected from the rich of that locality.[77] This aspect of the system performs a valuable role in promoting social cohesion. It serves as a visible demonstration of the spirit of oneness of people residing together in a certain area and of the concern felt for those in need on the part of those in a position to help.

Notes and References

1. The Qur'ān states: 'It is not fitting for a believer, man or woman, when a matter has been decided by God and His apostle, to have any option about their decision. If anyone disobeys God and His apostle, he is indeed on a clearly wrong path' (33: 36).

2. *Ijtihād* is a very carefully exercised process of reasoning which has its own set of rules and principles which keep it within the bounds of the fundamentals of Islam. For some details on the subject, see Said Ramaḍan, *Islamic Law: Its Scope and Equity* (London: Macmillan, 1961).

3. The Qur'ān states: 'O ye who believe! When the call is heard for the prayer of the day of congregation, haste unto the remembrance of Allah and leave your trading. That is better for you if ye did but know. And when the prayer is ended, then disperse in the land and seek of Allah's bounty, and remember Allah much, that ye may be successful' (62: 9–10).

4. Qur'ān, 34: 39.

5. Qur'ān, 78: 9–11.

6. Qur'ān, 7: 10; 14: 34; 15: 19–20.

7. See *Sunan Ibn Mājah,* (Riyadh: Sharikah at-Ṭibā'ah al-'Arabīyah as-Sa'ūdīyah, 1984), Vol. 2, p. 7.

8. *Ibid.,* p. 5.

9. See al-Bukhārī, *al-Jāmi' al-Ṣaḥīḥ* (Maktabah al-Riyāḍ al-Ḥadīthah, 1981), Vol. 2, p. 320.

10. For many sayings of the Prophet relevant in this context, see the chapter on *Zakāh* in Walī al-Dīn al-Tabrīzī, *Mishkāt al-Maṣābīḥ* (Damascus: al-Maktab al-Islāmī, ed. M. Nāṣir al-Dīn al-Albānī, A.H. 1381).

11. 'Allah it is Who hath made the sea of service unto you that the ships may run thereon by His command, and that ye may seek of His bounty, and that haply ye may be thankful. And hath made of service unto you whatsoever is in the heavens and whatsoever is in the earth; it is all from Him. Lo! herein verily are portents for people who reflect' (45: 12–13). See also 14: 32–3; 16: 12–14; and 22: 65.

12. Both the Qur'ān and the *Sunnah* emphasize the importance of acquiring knowledge. The very first revelation in the Qur'ān relates to acquisition of knowledge. It reads: 'Read: In the name of thy Lord Who createth, createth man from a clot. Read: And thy Lord is the Most

Bounteous, Who teacheth by the pen, teacheth man that which he knew not' (96: 1–5). According to the Prophet, 'acquisition of knowledge is compulsory for every Muslim.' See *Sunan Ibn Mājah, op. cit.*, Vol. 1, p. 48.

13. Early Islamic history is an exemplification of this view. The Prophet and the Caliphs in the early Islamic period never resorted to regimentation to solve economic problems.

14. On the basis of a saying of the Prophet quoted in *Sunan Ibn Mājah, op. cit.*, Vol. 2, p. 68, that 'All Muslims are partners in grass, water, and fire', the jurists have identified forests; pastures; unowned, unused land; and water flowing in the rivers and sea as the chief items falling under state domain.

15. One of the most lucid enunciations of this doctrine is contained in the following verse: 'Believe in Allah and His messenger, and spend of that whereof He hath made you trustees, and such of you as believe and spend (aright), theirs will be a great reward' (Qur'ān, 57: 7).

16. There is some discussion in juristic literature about the principles that should govern state regulation of private enterprise. An eminent jurist, Ibn Taimīyah, says: 'The principle is to secure greater social benefits *(maṣāliḥ)* and to abolish injury *(mafāsid)* or minimize it. When a situation arises where realization of one kind of benefit means the loss of another, then the greater benefit must be acquired in preference to the lesser. Conversely, the greater loss or injury must be avoided by tolerating a lesser one.' See 'Abdul 'Aẓīm Iṣlāḥi, *Economic Concepts of Ibn Taimīyah* (Leicester: The Islamic Foundation, 1988), pp. 180–1.

17. The details of Islam's social security system are given in a later section of this chapter.

18. Part of a verse reads as follows: 'Allah desireth for you ease; He desireth not hardship for you' (2: 185).

19. In the case of developing countries with abundant manpower, for example, employment-promoting policies would include adoption of labour-intensive techniques of production and encouragement of small-scale and cottage industries.

20. The role of Islamically-oriented monetary and fiscal policies in expanding employment opportunities and restraining income inequalities is discussed later in this chapter.

21. Qur'ān, 4: 29.

22. For details of the institution of *ḥisbah,* see Ibn Taimīyah, *Al-Ḥisbah fī al-Islām* (Cairo: Dār al-Sha'b, 1976).

23. The Prophet made an exception to this rule in the case of *bay' salam* which represented a contract of sale involving immediate payment of the price against promise of future delivery of goods subject to the condition that the quality and the nature of the article for sale, the time

and place of delivery, and the price are clearly defined at the time of making the contract of such sale. The exception was made particularly keeping in view the problems of poor agricultural producers.

24. Man has been advised to pray: 'My Lord! increase me in knowledge' (Qur'ān, 20: 114).

25. It is recorded by scholars that what is meant by 'water' here are the natural resources of water which have not been dug by man, like rivers, lakes, springs, and torrential streams. 'Herbage' stands for grass, herbs, and plants which grow on their own. 'Fire' means trees of the forest and thickets which are used as firewood.

26. Whether agricultural land can also be added to this list has been the subject of some discussion. However, jurists through the ages are agreed that Islam does not disallow private ownership of agricultural land. Private ownership of land was a recognized institution in the pre-Islamic world, yet there is no indication in the Qur'ān disapproving this institution. When the Prophet established the first Islamic state in Madinah, a large number of Muslims owned agricultural lands. The Prophet not only approved this but also allotted new lands to individuals.

27. Qur'ān, 4: 29.

28. The Qur'ān says: ' . . . Eat and drink, but be not prodigal. Lo! He loveth not the prodigals' (7: 31).

29. The Prophet disapproved the leaving of one's arable land idle by saying: 'Let him who owns land cultivate it himself; if he does not cultivate it himself, let him have his brother cultivate it.' See al-Mundhirī, *Mukhtaṣar Ṣaḥīḥ Muslim* (Kuwait: al-Dār al-Kuwaitiyah liṭṭibā'ah wan Nashr wa'l-Tawzī', 1969), Vol. 2, p. 17.

30. The Prophet is reported to have said that 'No harm, and no inflicting of harm'. See *Sunan Ibn Mājah, op. cit.,* Vol. 2, p. 44.

31. Qur'ān, 51: 19 and 70: 24–5.

32. The details are given in a subsequent part of this chapter under the heading of Islam's social security system.

33. For details, see note 62.

34. For the views of some scholars on this issue, see 'Abd al-Qādir 'Audah, *al-Māl wa'l-ḥukm fi'l-Islām* (Jeddah: ad-Dār as-Sa'ūdīyah bin-Nashr, 1969), pp. 46–9. 'Abd al-Salām al-'Abbādī, *Al-Milkiyyah fī al-Sharī'ah al-Islāmiyyah* (Amman: Maktabat al-Aqṣā, 1974), Vol. 2, pp. 398–420, and Muḥammad Quṭb, *Al-Insān Bayn al-Māddiyyah wa al-Islām* (Cairo: 'Īsā al-Bābī al-Ḥalabī, 1965), pp. 160–8 and 200–1.

35. 'And when kinsfolk and orphans and the needy are present at the division (of the heritage), bestow on them therefrom and speak kindly unto them' (4: 8).

36. 'O ye who believe! Observe your duty to Allah, and give up what remaineth (due to you) from usury, if ye are (in truth) believers. And if ye do not, then be warned of war (against you) from Allah and His messenger. And if ye repent, then ye have your principal (without interest). Wrong not, and ye shall not be wronged' (2: 278–9).

37. See, for example, Ibn Taimīyah, *Majmū' Fatāwā Shaikh al-Islām Aḥmad ibn Taimīyah* (Riyadh: Al-Riyad Press, 1971), Vol. 29, pp. 55–125.

38. For a detailed account of differing viewpoints of jurists on this issue see 'Abd al-Raḥmān Al-Jazīrī, *Kitāb al-fiqh 'alā al-madhāhib al-Arba'ah* (Cairo: Al-Maktabah al-tijāriyyah al-kubrā, 1969), Vol. 3, pp. 1–33.

39. Qur'ān, 26: 183.

40. The Prophet is reported to have said, 'A man has not earned better income than that which is from his own labour.' See *Sunan Ibn Mājah, op. cit.,* Vol. 2, p. 5.

41. Most of these sayings are found in the collection of *aḥādīth* relating to the treatment of slaves but the spirit underlying them is of general applicability. One of the sayings speaks of the subordinates being 'entitled to at least moderately good food and clothing'. See Aḥmad Ibn Ḥanbal, *Musnad al-Imām Aḥmad* (Beirut: Dār Sādir, 1969), Vol. 2, p. 247, and Mālik ibn Anas, *al-Muwaṭṭa'* (Beirut: Dār al-Nafais, 1973), p. 695.

42. In the *aḥādīth* referred to in the previous note, mention is also made of the subordinates 'not being burdened with tasks beyond their powers'. This provides a basis for fixation of maximum work hours for various types of labour and regulation of other working conditions.

43. 'Those who spend their wealth for the cause of Allah and afterward make not reproach and injury to follow that which they have spent; their reward is with their Lord and there shall be no fear come upon them, neither shall they grieve' (2: 262).

44. 'Who is it that will lend unto Allah a goodly loan so that He may give it increase manifold?' (Qur'ān, 2: 245).

45. Apart from *zakāh,* it is also obligatory on Muslims to help the poor on the occasion of the festival of *'Īd al-fitr* by making a specific contribution in kind or money. According to the majority of jurists, this contribution is one *ṣā'* of the staple food of the country, which comes to 2.175 kg. in terms of wheat.

46. 'Hast thou observed him who belieth religion? That is he who repelleth the orphan and urgeth not the feeding of the needy' (107: 1–3).

47. Qur'ān, 2: 219.

48. This was the view, for example, of Abu Dharr, a companion of the Prophet. However, this view was not shared by most of the Prophet's companions.

49. 'Spend your wealth for the cause of Allah, and be not cast by your own hands to ruin; and do good. Lo! Allah loveth the beneficent' (2: 195).

50. This shows that the Islamic vision of a just socio-economic order contains the notion of interdependent utility functions as an integral part of it.

51. For detailed information on *waqf,* see Muṣṭafā Sibā'ī, *Min Rawā'i' Ḥaḍāratinā* (Beirut: Dār al-Qur'ān al-Karīm, 1980), pp. 173–82.

52. For more details, see Muhammad Anas Zarqa, 'Islamic Distributive Schemes', in Munawar Iqbal (ed.), *Distributive Justice and Need Fulfilment in an Islamic Economy* (Islamabad: International Institute of Islamic Economics; Leicester: The Islamic Foundation, 1988), pp. 163–216.

53. The basic features of the levy known as *zakāh* are given later in this chapter. See pp. 48–52.

54. For a brief description of the fiscal system in the early Islamic period, see Ziāuddin Aḥmad, 'Public Finance in Islam', IMF Working Paper (WP/89/68).

55. This, in essence, is a summary of the extended discussion in juristic literature on the subject of taxation in an Islamic economy. For the views of a number of jurists on this subject, see Yūsuf Al-Qarḍāwī, *Fiqh al-Zakāh* (Beirut: Mu'assasat al-Risālah, 1973), pp. 1072–105.

56. These and other similar maxims are found in the work of many jurists. See, for example, the enunciation of such maxims in *Mājalla.* For Arabic text with commentary, see 'Alī Ḥayder, *Durar al-Ḥukkām Sharh Majallat al-Aḥkām* (Beirut: n.d.). For an English translation, see C. R. Tyser, *The Majelle* (Lahore: Law Publishing Company, 1980).

57. It must be clarified at this stage that the responsibility of satisfying the basic needs of all citizens rests on the society as a whole. There are several institutional mechanisms that exist in a truly Islamic society which help in the need-fulfilment of poorer sections of society, and if these are operative the residual responsibility of the state in this respect is greatly reduced. Moreover, it would be essential that a pragmatic view is taken of the standard of need-fulfilment keeping in view the general economic conditions and average standard of living in a country so that this responsibility is financially manageable.

58. See *Banking for the Poor: Alleviating Poverty through Credit Assistance to the Poorest Micro-Entrepreneurs in Developing Countries,* Report of the Select Committee on Hunger, U.S. House of Representatives (Washington: U.S. Government Printing Office, May 1986).

59. For a detailed exposition of Islamic financing techniques, see M. U. Chapra, *Towards a Just Monetary System* (Leicester: The Islamic Foundation, 1985).

60. Qur'ān, 7: 85.

61. Qur'ān, 8: 75, 17: 26, 30: 38.

62. Jurists are generally agreed that legal compulsion can be used for the provision of maintenance support in the following cases: (a) to a wife from her husband irrespective of her own financial position, (b) to poor and needy parents from their sons, (c) to minor sons and daughters, unmarried or widowed or divorced adult daughter in need of assistance, and adult son incapable of earning his own living, from his father. There is a difference of opinion among jurists in regard to the use of legal compulsion in the case of other relatives. Many jurists are of the view that legal compulsion can be used to force the affluent persons to provide maintenance support to all those persons who figure in the inheritance scheme of Islam. Thus, according to this view, brothers, sisters, grandfather, grandmother, grandsons, granddaughters and certain other relatives are also entitled to maintenance support. For a comprehensive discussion of the views of various jurists on the subject of obligatory assistance to poor relatives, see 'Abd al-Raḥmān al-Jazīrī, *Kitāb al-fiqh 'alā al-madhāhib al-Arba'ah* (Cairo: Al-Maktabah al-tijāriyyah al-kubrā) and Aḥmad Ibn Ibrāhīm Ibrāhīm, *Niẓām al-Nafaqāt fī al-Sharī'ah al-Islāmīyah* (Cairo: al-Maṭba'ah al-Salafīyah).

63. The responsibility of an Islamic state to set up a social security system which ensures fulfilment of the basic needs of all citizens is inferred from the texts in the Qur'ān, sayings of the Prophet and the practice in the early Islamic period. See pp. 17–19 of this book.

64. Qur'ān, 107: 1–3.

65. Qur'ān, 51: 19.

66. *Zakāh,* in its literal sense, means 'purification' and 'growth'. According to the Islamic beliefs, as enunciated in the Qur'ān and the *Sunnah*, payment of *zakāh* purifies one's soul and leads to increase in material welfare in this world and growth of religious merit in the Hereafter.

67. Qur'ān, 9: 103.

68. Qur'ān, 9: 60.

69. For a thorough review of juristic discussion on the subject, see Yūsuf al-Qarḍāwī, *Fiqh al-Zakāh, op. cit.,* pp. 544–78.

70. For a detailed discussion of these issues, see *ibid.,* pp. 489–510.

71. For details, see *ibid.,* pp. 168–237.

72. There is a difference of opinion among jurists on the point whether the *niṣāb* must be complete every moment through the year or only at the beginning and end of the year. Similarly there are differences on the treatment to be accorded to increments in assets during the course of the year. See the chapter on *zakāh* in 'Abd al-Raḥmān al-Jazīrī, *Kitāb al-fiqh 'alā al-madhāhib al-Arba'ah, op. cit.*

73. Two such studies relate to Syria and Sudan. For details, see Muḥammad Anas Zarqa, 'Islamic Distributive Schemes', *op. cit.*

74. The implementation of an Islamic fiscal system requires the adoption of a two-budget concept. See in this connection, Ziāuddin Aḥmad, 'Public Finance in Islam', *op. cit.*

75. See al-Tirmidhī, *al-Jāmi' aṣ-Ṣaḥīḥ* (Beirut: Dār al-Fikr, 1974), Vol. 2, p. 85.

76. One of these sayings is recorded as follows: 'Each one of you is a shepherd, responsible for his flock: the head of the state for his (people) and the one who has the position of shepherd in his family for (the welfare) of his (family)'. See al-Bukhārī, *al-Jāmi' al-Ṣaḥīḥ, op. cit.*, Vol. 3, p. 438.

77. A large number of sayings of the Prophet stress this feature of Islam's social security system. A famous saying of the Prophet is: 'Tell them that there is a charity due upon them to be taken from their rich and to be given back to their poor'. *Ibid.*, Vol. 2, pp. 271–2.

CHAPTER 3

The Distinctiveness of the Islamic Approach

Every human society employs the resources available to it to produce a stream of output which is distributed in some manner among its members. Equity and justice in the arrangements governing production of goods and services and distribution of gross national product have been the focus of attention throughout human history. A more or less unequal income distribution, however measured, can be observed in all societies at all times. Ideas and policy prescriptions on how to tackle the problem of poverty and inequalities of income and wealth occupy a wide spectrum. They range from advocacy of allowing full play to free market forces and least interference with private enterprise to complete state control over production and distribution. This chapter delineates the salient features of some of the leading approaches to issues of poverty and income distribution in the past and the present, and ends with an identification of the distinctive features of the Islamic approach in this matter.

For a long time in human history, production and distribution processes were largely governed by tradition. In the tradition-bound societies of the hoary past, custom and heredity were the main factors which determined division of labour as well as the distribution of the fruits of labour. The ancient hunting and gathering societies were perforce highly egalitarian societies as they eked out a day-to-day existence through individual effort, and were incapable of producing any appreciable economic surplus which could be appropriated by any particular group.[1] These were followed by simple horticultural societies which once flourished throughout most of Europe, the Middle East, and South and East Asia. These were normally larger, more productive, and less egalitarian.[2] However, inequalities were far from pronounced as land was available in abundance and most material necessities were readily available to all.

The first evidence of marked inequalities in income and wealth in human history is found in the advanced horticultural societies which had their beginnings in the Middle East more than six thousand years ago and which subsequently spread to the five major continents.[3] On account of the technological advances in horticulture, it became possible to produce more than one's subsistence requirements. The surplus was largely appropriated by tribal chiefs who lived in relatively greater comfort and also maintained a retinue of dependent officials. The institution of slavery also made its appearance in this period. The exercise of royal favour by tribal chiefs or kings gave rise to a privileged nobility. At the bottom were the great majority of common people, who produced the surplus on which the more privileged classes depended for a life of ease and comfort. Money, in the form of cowrie shells, and cattle were the new types of tangible assets which facilitated both the accumulation of wealth and its transfer from generation to generation.

The agrarian societies, which succeeded the advanced horticultural societies, were characterized by increased specialization and greater division of labour. The development of specialization necessarily implied the development of trade and commerce, and the emergence of a distinct merchant class. The agrarian societies in most areas evinced a good deal of social inequality. The agrarian rulers enjoyed proprietary rights in virtually all the land and businesses in their realm. The exercise of proprietary rights, through the collection of taxes, tribute money, rent, and services provided the chief sources of income for most agrarian rulers. A small minority, estimated by some scholars to be no more than 2 per cent of the population,[4] shared the responsibilities of government with them. Frequently rulers granted members of the governing class vast landed estates or the incomes from them. According to certain research studies, 'it appears that the governing classes of agrarian societies probably received at least a quarter of the national income of most agrarian states, and that the governing class and ruler together usually received not less than half. In some instances their combined income may have approached two-thirds of the total.'[5] The peasants, who formed a substantial majority of the population, lived very nearly at subsistence level. They were also subject to corvee or forced labour. In many regions, peasants were bound to the soil by law and custom. The feudal lords held them in almost complete bondage, a state of affairs known in economic history as serfdom.

The economic plight of the poor in the agrarian societies drew protests from social reformers of the time.[6] The religious precepts of the leading faiths of Judaism, Christianity, and Islam provided a firm basis for an ethical criticism of the then existing economic order. The humanizing impact of religion varied from century to century and area to area. The practical implementation of Islamic teachings in the Arabian peninsula and adjoining lands in the early Islamic period, which included the introduction of Islam's social security system, brought about a striking transformation in the lot of the poor. The Muslim societies retained a pronounced egalitarian bias for a considerable time[7] but, subsequently with the relative neglect of Islamic teachings both on the part of the rulers and the ruled, the earlier commitment toward the amelioration of the sufferings of the poor waned considerably and the state-organized social security system also fell into disuse.

The Middle Ages saw a growing discontent of the peasantry with their lot and a constant struggle to free themselves from the clutches of serfdom. Historians have recorded thousands of peasant uprisings in this period in the countries of Europe and elsewhere which were ruthlessly suppressed.[8] With the passage of time, however, economic growth and market expansion led to significant changes in agricultural tenures and class relations in agrarian societies. The enclosures movement in England and other European countries provided a powerful impetus for the dissolution of feudal ties and the formation of new relationships in a more market-oriented society. The enclosures process resulted in dispossessing a large number of peasants and converting them into landless labourers. Legal changes in many countries undermined communal agricultural arrangements and freed workers to do wage labour. With the gradual urbanization of medieval life and technological developments leading to the Industrial Revolution, the growing working class began to displace the peasantry as the single largest occupational class. This structural change in the economies of countries undergoing an industrial revolution failed, however, to bring about any marked improvement in the poverty situation of large sections of the population for quite a long time.[9]

The onset of the Industrial Revolution in European countries was accompanied by a strong belief in the virtues of a free-market economy as epitomized in the *laissez-faire* philosophy. The essence of this philosophy is that free play of competitive forces in both commodity and factor markets, unimpeded by the influence of any public authority, is the best recipe for economic progress. Competitive market capitalism is the best known economic system generated by the *laissez-faire* doctrine. The basic features of competitive market capitalism are individual ownership and control of the means of production, the pursuit of individual economic gain as the driving force in economic decisions, and a competitive market price system as the dominant institutional mechanism for resource allocation and income distribution. During the late eighteenth and greater part of the nineteenth century, the organization and practices of almost all the European countries and the United States roughly approximated the characteristics of the competitive market capitalism model. Thc economic organization of many countries in Asia, Africa, and elsewhere which became subject to colonial domination by European powers also exhibited the same characteristics.

The growth of competitive market capitalism in its early phases was marked by tremendous social suffering. Though the countries undergoing an industrial revolution achieved a remarkable increase in gross domestic product, the gains from development were very inequitably distributed. The wages paid to industrial labour were just sufficient for mere subsistence. The unorganized labourers had to work for long hours in unhygenic surroundings. The living conditions were miserable. The lot of the unemployed was even worse. The dominance of *laissez-faire* philosophy gave rise to a callous disregard for the plight of the poor.[10] Leading economists of the time dealt with labour in their treatises as just another commodity whose price (wage) was determined by the free play of market forces of supply and demand.[11] The general attitude toward poverty in those times is portrayed in the following words in a recent work:

> . . . the poor were looked upon as objects of pity or scorn, depending on the humanity of the observer, but never as subjects for economic uplift through social action. Some looked upon the poor as random sufferers of bad luck . . . Others thought that the poor had only themselves to blame for their low estate . . . Malthus (a famous economist) argued for the elimination of even (the) limited form of poor relief (that existed at the time), and advised that the family head should be taught . . . that he had no claim of right on society for the smallest portion of food, beyond that which his labour would fairly purchase . . . While Malthus wanted to stop poor relief to clear the path for starvation and thereby validate his circular logic that the poor were superfluous, others saw poverty as a spur to labour efficiency and an inducement to social conformity . . . The same negative attitudes were imported into the United States, where observers saw poverty as the result of misconduct or individual misfortune but never as a widespread economic affliction resulting from the operation of the socio-economic system itself and requiring social action to remedy.[12]

Notwithstanding the dominance of *laissez-faire* philosophy in that period some voices were raised against the inequalities of the system based on this philosophy, and sporadic reform measures were taken from time to time. In England, for example, a notable development took place in 1795 in the form of the Speenhamland Law which provided that subsidies in aid of wages should be granted in accordance with a scale dependent upon the price of bread, so that a minimum income should be assured to the poor irrespective of their earnings.[13] However, this law had a short-lived existence and was abolished in 1834.

The twentieth century represents a great watershed in human history in that issues of poverty and income distribution have become matters of foremost concern throughout the world. The nineteenth century had witnessed growing dissatisfaction with policies of *laissez-faire* which had failed to provide an effective solution to problems of poverty and income distribution. The *laissez-faire* philosophy has been almost totally abandoned throughout the world during the course of the twentieth century. It has given way to two broad approaches of economic policy-making which are described as 'socialism' and 'managed capitalism' in the current economic literature. Though the two approaches differ in substantive ways they both represent attempts at social reform through active state intervention.

The professed aims of socialism are abolition of poverty and the creation of a social service state, a drastic reduction in inequalities of income and wealth and economic planning for full employment and stability. According to Karl Marx, the most reputed exponent of the socialist doctrine, these objectives can only be attained if capitalism is first overthrown. Marx believed that the capitalist system was riddled with inherent contradictions which would inevitably lead to its demise. Marx did not doubt the capacity of a capitalist system to produce an increasing quantity of goods and services but felt that due to the capitalists' exploitation of labour, the conditions of the masses would become so intolerable that they would rise in revolt and overthrow the capitalist system. Capitalism would be replaced by socialism under which all means of production would be nationalized, all private incomes except wages would be eliminated, and workers would receive in wages the full value of what they produced less whatever was reserved for social saving. The production and distribution of goods and services would be undertaken in a planned manner by state agencies. Socialism, according to Marx, would eventually give way to communism under which the state would whither away and individuals would lead a communal existence, drawing upon the community's income according to need rather than according to the individual's ability to produce.[14]

Marx's vision of the establishment of a socialist society through a revolutionary overthrow of the capitalist order by workers is not shared by all socialist thinkers. The Fabian socialists, for example, believe that a socialist society can be brought into existence through the democratic will of the people who are dissatisfied with the working of a capitalist system.[15]

The proponents of 'managed capitalism' are of the view that the inadequacies of *laissez-faire* capitalism can be overcome with appropriate state intervention without giving up the fundamental features of a capitalist system. They recognize that there are circumstances in which the working of the free-market mechanism may fail to achieve the social goals of a society. The recurrent cycles of booms and slumps that were experienced by the industrializing countries in the nineteenth century had already shaken belief in the basic postulate of classical economics that a competitive market economy had in-built self-correcting mechanisms to avoid prolonged periods of booms and slumps. The Great Depression of the 1930s dealt a final blow to such a belief and threatened the survival of capitalism as an economic system. Keynesian macroeconomics, which substituted a positive role for government monetary and fiscal policies in place of *laissez-faire,* was one of the saviours of capitalism. Economists identified a number of other cases, called market failures, where the market system, left to itself, may not operate to best social advantage. A proper role for government to deal with such market failures also became part of the new economic thinking. Cognizance was also taken of the problems posed by persistent poverty and glaring inequalities of income and wealth, and increasing attention was given to finding ways and means of a more equitable sharing of gains from development under a regime of managed capitalism.

The rise of political liberalism in the economically advanced countries of the West has been an important factor in increased attention being given to problems of poverty and income inequalities. After the turn of the century, and particularly in the period following the Great Depression, governments in these countries have no longer been willing to allow market forces alone to determine the levels of employment, production, and income. They have found it necessary to intervene in economic affairs on quite a wide front. State intervention has taken the form of varying degrees of public ownership of the means of production, active use of tax policy to reduce inequalities of income and wealth, and sizeable programmes for public welfare and social security. The pronounced redistributive bias in the economic policies of these countries and a palpable concern for the lot of the poor has earned them the title of 'welfare states'.

The developing countries of the Third World, which contain the largest number of the world's poor, have followed varying strategies for poverty alleviation and reduction in inequalities of income and wealth. 'Managed capitalism' has provided the basic framework for the conduct of economic policies in most of these countries. Generally speaking, countries of the Third World following the 'managed capitalism' model lack a social security system of the type found in industrially advanced countries. Some of them have no social security system worth the name while others have social security systems which provide limited benefits to particular categories of the population. Some developing countries have chosen to follow the socialist model of development.

From the viewpoint of economic management, and particularly from the viewpoint of policies pursued for alleviation of poverty and reduction in inequalities of income and wealth, countries of the present-day world can be roughly classified in three broad groups: (1) capitalist countries with well developed social security systems, (2) capitalist countries without any social security system or relatively less developed social security systems, and (3) socialist countries. It is noteworthy that countries with well developed social security systems are all high-income developed countries. None of the low- and middle-income capitalist countries has a well developed social security system. It is also important to note that even among countries considered capitalist and countries considered socialist, there are wide variations in the types of economic policies pursued and patterns of income distribution.

Eradication of poverty and achievement of a highly egalitarian pattern of income distribution are the major goals of socialism. In the economic theory of socialism, all means of production are supposed to be under the ownership and control of the state. The allocation of resources is supposed to be accomplished by administrative decisions rather than by a market mechanism. Economic coordination among various state agencies is supposed to be achieved through a system of comprehensive planning based primarily on material resources budgeting. The elimination of capitalist private ownership of the means of production is expected to bring about an equitable pattern of income distribution. The socialist model of development was first introduced in Russia in 1917. Since then the country has experimented with different strategies of socialist development. The early period was marked by nationalization of banks and major industries, collectivization of farms, use of state power to exterminate the more affluent land owning peasants (the 'kulaks'), regimentation of labour and emphasis on development of heavy industry. The era of comprehensive planning began in 1928, and since then successive five-year plans have been used to mould the pace and direction of economic change. The policies pursued have succeeded in making the Soviet Union one of the two major superpowers of the world and a highly industrialized country. The use of comprehensive planning has enabled the country to provide its people with a high degree of job and income security. The social security system provides free education, free medical service, and old age pensions. Information concerning changes in income distribution in the Soviet Union is rather scanty. As would be expected in a fully socialist state, abolition of income from large property holdings has resulted in a significant reduction in inequalities of income and wealth. However, considerable differences still exist between top and bottom incomes. According to one analyst, the span between the lowest and highest incomes in the Soviet Union in 1971 was 1:3.5, and almost one third of the families had incomes below the poverty line.[16]

Apart from the Soviet Union, the socialist model of development has been in operation in a number of East European countries in the period following the Second World War. Till 1953, these countries were very closely tied to the Soviet Union and their economic policies were almost identical to those followed in the Soviet Union. Subsequently, they have pursued more independent policies. Some of them adopted a more flexible system of allocating resources and making production decisions.[17] Two East European countries, Hungary and Yugoslavia, even introduced certain marketization principles within an overall socialist framework. Yugoslavia also made a significant departure from the centralized system in the 1950s by introducing workers' control of collective enterprises.[18] Though data on changes in the pattern of income distribution in East European countries are scanty, the limited information available shows that the share of the poorest 20 per cent of the population in these countries ranged from 6.6 per cent to 11.2 per cent while the share of the richest 20 per cent ranged from 34.3 per cent to 40.7 per cent.[19] It is also reported that the policies pursued in these countries have helped to reduce and in some cases eliminate the worst forms of poverty and degradation.[20]

Among other socialist countries, China deserves special mention. Prior to the revolution in 1949, China was essentially a feudal land with glaring inequalities of income and wealth. Since then a policy of balanced growth has led to considerable industrial advancement. At first, China had a highly centralized economic system with collectivized agriculture and tightly controlled industry. However, the rural commune system was reformed in the 1960s to restore to some extent the material incentives that had been lost as a result of the policy of collectivization. In the 1980s, state industrial enterprises were given more autonomy in an effort to improve their productive efficiency. More recent reforms have sought to promote diversified forms of economic organization, with some state enterprises leased to individuals or collectives. An active policy is being pursued to attract foreign investors for joint ventures or exclusive investments in enterprises necessary for the modernization of the economy. As a result of the emphasis on limiting wage and salary differentials, income distribution in China is more equal than in many other socialist countries.[21] Though the country still has a low per capita income, the distributional policies have sought to ensure sufficiency of food intake and a wide range of social services.[22]

The socialist philosophy has influenced economic decision-making in a number of developing countries. However, only a few of them have the essential attributes of a socialist economic order. According to one analyst, only six countries of the Third World can be classified as 'indisputably' socialist. These are China, Cuba, Kampuchea, Mongolia, North Korea, and Vietnam.[23] Available evidence shows that, compared to other developing countries, they have recorded a better performance in respect of poverty alleviation and reduction in inequalities of income and wealth.[24]

Though the socialist countries have achieved significant results in achieving a more equitable pattern of income distribution, they are beset with a number of problems which have forced quite a few of them to make significant departures from the orthodox socialist model of development. Falling growth rates, slow pace of technological change, bureaucratic inefficiency in the operation of state-run industries, and consumer discontent with the short and irregular supplies of goods of everyday use have been the major areas of concern. Despite many diversities in the individual circumstances of various countries, something of a common pattern of economic reform has emerged. This consists of a movement away from a tightly controlled, centrally planned economy to a decentralized market-oriented economy, improved enterprise and plant management, more effective harnessing of individual incentives, and more concern for consumer welfare. At the same time, in many socialist countries, people have shown dissatisfaction with the authoritarian nature of their political system which has denied them the civil and political liberties found in pluralistic democratic societies. This found the most concrete expression in the political upheaval witnessed in several East European countries during the later part of 1989 and the first quarter of 1990. The economies of these countries are presently in a state of flux and the course events will take in the future is as yet uncertain.

In the high income capitalist countries, the current concern with social security and egalitarianism is in marked contrast to the rigours of capitalist development in the 18th and 19th centuries. Actually, the faint beginning of welfare statism in some of these countries can be traced back to the last quarter of the 19th century when, as a defensive reaction to the growth of socialist ideas, Bismarck of Germany sponsored health insurance and old age insurance schemes. Another precursor of the modern welfare state was the social welfare programme of the Liberal Government in the United Kingdom. Developed in 1908, the programme included social insurance for health and unemployment, old age pensions, and assistance to low income workers through statutory fixing of minimum wages.[25] The large-scale unemployment during the Great Depression of the 1930s, which constituted a threat to the survival of capitalism, spurred the rise of the welfare state in Western countries. After 1929, the Social Democratic parties became major factors in the political systems of a number of Scandinavian countries and, under their influence and guidance, economic policies in these countries were given a pronounced welfare orientation. The political complexion of the ruling parties in other advanced capitalist countries has been an important factor in setting the pace of social welfare policies in different time periods. However, all the high income capitalist countries have well developed social security systems in place to provide protection from the insecurities of a capitalist system.[26]

An important characteristic of the social security programmes of advanced capitalist countries is that they are often designed for all citizens, regardless of their individual financial position. Available evidence shows that these programmes have done a lot to alleviate poverty. However, even in the most advanced countries, poverty has not been eradicated completely. In the United States, for example, according to the latest annual survey of the Census Bureau, about 13 per cent of the population was below the officially defined poverty line in 1988. According to a well researched study about poverty profile in four advanced countries,[27] about 10 per cent of the population in these countries was below the poverty line in 1973.

With the transformation in the nature of capitalism during the present century, a fair sharing of the national income has become a widely held national goal in advanced capitalist countries. However, nations have different perspectives of how far they should go in securing this goal. A 1976 study of size distribution of post-tax personal income in ten industrialized countries by the Organization for Economic Cooperation and Development revealed that the United Kingdom and other countries such as Norway and Sweden, which followed more egalitarian policies, had a much less post-tax income inequality than certain other countries like the United States, France, and Germany.[28] It appears to many analysts that even after the advent of 'managed capitalism', the economic policies pursued in many advanced countries have not generated forces causing a significant reduction in inequalities of income and wealth.[29] According to a detailed study of trends in income distribution in a number of countries, the top 20 per cent of income groups had a share exceeding 50 per cent of total income in two advanced countries, and these groups had a share falling between 40 per cent and 50 per cent of total income in 11 countries.[30] According to the same study, the bottom 20 per cent of income groups had an average of 5.5 per cent of total income in the 17 developed countries included in the study.[31]

The largest mass of poverty-stricken people live in what is known as the Third World. Colonialism was an important factor in keeping the vast majority of people poor in Third World countries under foreign domination. After gaining independence, developing countries have been confronted with 'the revolution of rising expectations' and they are engaged in a valiant effort to overcome economic backwardness and poverty to fulfil these expectations. Some of these countries have followed a socialist model of development while others have followed the path of managed capitalism. The development experience of socialist countries has already been commented upon. Economic development in the capitalist framework has yielded mixed results. Some developing countries have achieved significant success in reducing the numbers and proportions of people living in poverty and in improving the pattern of income distribution. Development of the type experienced by a large number of countries, however, has not made much of an impact on poverty and has in fact resulted in a worsening of income distribution.[32]

Available evidence shows that in the period after the Second World War developing countries have recorded a resounding success in their efforts to raise the growth rates of their gross national product. It is reported that 'GNP per capita of the developing countries grew at an average rate of 3.4 per cent per annum during 1950–75 or 3 per cent if the People's Republic of China is excluded. This was faster than either the developed or the developing nations had grown in any comparable period prior to 1950, and exceeded both official goals and private expectations.'[33] However, in a large number of countries, growth was accompanied by increasing inequalities of income and wealth. In one of the research studies,[34] which examined data relating to 43 non-socialist countries in the post-World War II period, it was found that as economic growth proceeded, the share of the bottom 60 per cent of the people fell relatively. It was also found that in the poorer countries the income of the bottom 40 per cent had fallen absolutely as well, that is, these people had less income in absolute terms at the end of two decades of development than they had in the beginning. Cross-sectional data about the pattern of income distribution in a number of countries assembled by the World Bank some time back showed glaring income inequalities.[35] According to these figures, the share of the poorest 20 per cent households in total income ranged from 1.9 per cent to 7.5 per cent in the 14 countries covered by the study while the share of the 20 per cent richest households ranged from 43.4 per cent to 66.6 per cent. Information about the quantitative dimensions of poverty is rather scanty. There are very few estimates of the 'poverty gap' and estimates about the number of people below the 'poverty line' differ from study to study. According to one study,[36] 35.6 per cent of the population in the nine Asian countries covered in the study lived below the poverty line. The percentage of the population living below the poverty line in the seven African countries covered in the study was about 36 per cent while the corresponding figure in the case of 15 Latin American countries was about 13 per cent. These averages conceal considerable inter-country variations. Thus, in the Asian countries, the proportion of the population living below the poverty line ranged between 1.21 and 41.33 per cent and in Latin American countries between 0.93 and 27.46 per cent.

The highly uneven performance of different countries in the alleviation of poverty and reduction in income inequalities has been the subject matter of extended discussion among economists and sociologists in recent years. Until the 1960s it was widely believed that the best hope of a speedy reduction in poverty was to concentrate on accelerating the overall rate of economic growth. However, analysis of the development experience of a number of countries showed that a high rate of growth provided no assurance that the benefits of growth would trickle down to the masses.[37] This has given rise to new thinking with regard to alternative strategies of development but so far there is no unanimity as to what is the best course to follow.

Some economists are of the view that there are certain systematic forces which govern changes in the pattern of income distribution as economic growth proceeds. The well-known 'U-hypothesis'[38] says that income distribution will worsen in the initial stages of growth but will improve afterwards. The reasoning behind this hypothesis is as follows. Economic growth involves a shift from traditional to modern sector activities. Inequality in the traditional sector is less than in the modern sector. As the modern sector expands with development, the increasing weight of the modern sector population means an increase in overall income inequalities. Later, in higher stages of growth, this trend is reversed as there is a larger flow of incomes to the lower income groups in the increasingly large modern sector. On the basis of this hypothesis, it is argued that the foremost concern of development strategy should be to press forward with the process of modernization without too much concern for the pattern of income distribution in the initial stages of growth. This approach, however, has lost considerable support in recent years. It has been pointed out that the 'U-hypothesis' is not a law of nature. It lacks a strong theoretical basis and pays insufficient attention to the role of policy in affecting the time path of inequality.[39] Many analysts have pointed out that the development strategy pursued and the resulting economic structure have far more influence on income distribution than per capita income, and the 'U-hypothesis' does not justify the pursuit of neutral income distribution policies as growth proceeds.[40]

A widely discussed development strategy with focus on income distribution issues has come to be known as 'redistribution with growth'. The essence of this strategy is to shift the emphasis of development from growth of output to a more equitable sharing of the benefits of growth. A policy framework for such a strategy had long been discussed in academic circles but the idea gained in popularity when the Development Research Center of the World Bank under Hollis Chenery came out with an elaborate study on the subject.[41] The main conclusion of the study was that an appreciable improvement in the lot of the bottom 40 per cent of the population over a sustained period of time is possible through a policy of redirection of the pattern of investment in their favour. Since low incomes result from the lack of physical capital, access to infrastructure, and a wide range of complementary inputs, government policy should be directed to overcoming these obstacles.

Another widely discussed approach for tackling the poverty problem is known as 'basic needs' approach. The essence of this approach is a definitive priority to the fulfilment of the basic needs of the poor. This approach was strongly articulated by the International Labour Organization (ILO) in the 1970s.[42] The ILO defined basic needs to include the 'minimum requirements of a family for private consumption', notably food, shelter and clothing, and 'essential services provided by and for the community at large, such as safe drinking water, sanitation, public transportation, and health and education facilities'. While outlining this approach, the ILO recognized that in most developing countries the goal of the fulfilment of basic needs could not be achieved without substantial redistribution of income and wealth.

Notwithstanding greater attention to issues of poverty and income distribution in developing countries during the past two decades or so, actual achievements have been disappointing. Although several countries have moved some way in adopting redistributive strategies of development, the change in policies has been far too limited to lead to any significant results.[43] The magnitude of the effort that is required to overcome the poverty problem can be judged from the results of the simulation exercises conducted by the ILO in the 1970s and published in 1976.[44] In one of these calculations, it was assumed that GNP will grow at a steady 6 per cent per annum and the population in different regions will grow in accordance with the 'low' estimate of the United Nations. It was found that to satisfy even the conservatively estimated basic needs within a period of 30 years, the share of the poorest 20 per cent of the population would have to more than double compared to what they were in 1970 in most regions of the developing world, and in the case of tropical Africa the share of the poor would have to increase 3–4 times.[45] The extent of redistribution that would be needed to meet basic needs would be even greater if the rate of growth in GNP is assumed to be less than 6 per cent per annum.

The debate on ways and means of tackling the problems of poverty and income distribution continues but it is now generally agreed that there can be no hope for eradication of poverty unless the development strategies are given a pronounced redistributive bias. Some analysts have expressed a great deal of pessimism about the likelihood of adoption of such strategies as they feel that it is very doubtful that upper income groups would be prepared to make the necessary sacrifice.[46] Others pin their hopes on the emergence of a 'coalition of interests' which sees some advantage in implementing a redistributive strategy, despite the fact that some sections of it stand to lose relatively thereby.[47] The work of international institutions like the World Bank and the IMF on development issues also points to the need for strong government commitment for an effective solution to the poverty problem.[48]

After the foregoing review of the leading approaches to issues of poverty and income distribution in the past and the present, it is proposed now to turn to an identification of the distinctive features of the Islamic approach in this matter. The policy framework for the eradication of poverty and reduction in inequalities of income and wealth, as deduced from Islamic teachings, has already been set out in the preceding chapter. The various components of this policy framework are finely welded together by certain divine concepts related directly to the basic social structure which implies a definite scheme of income distribution and redistribution within the society. If one looks for the distinguishing characteristics of the basic social structure, its dominant element is seen to lie in the concept of man's 'trusteeship'. Through this concept of trusteeship, Islam seeks to imbue its followers with a strong sense of responsibility for the welfare of everyone in the society. The essence of the concept of trusteeship is that God is the owner of everything that exists in the world, and what man holds by way of his possessions is in the nature of a trust to be discharged in accordance with God's will. When this concept settles in the psyche of human beings the way is cleared for the coming into being of a just and equitable socio-economic order. However, Islam does not confine itself only to a preaching of ethical principles. It uses the power of the state, to the extent considered necessary, to ensure justice in all human relations, and this includes economic justice in the sense of the society being free from poverty and socially disruptive inequalities of income and wealth. The guidelines for individual and state action are all derived from the Qur'ān and the Prophet's sayings and actions known as *sunnah*. The Islamic approach to the eradication of poverty and containment of inequalities of income and wealth within acceptable limits is thus a blend of ethical, socio-political and juridical elements, derived from religious sources, which sets it apart from other approaches which are not bound by any specific religious precepts.

The fact that the Islamic approach to eradication of poverty and reduction in inequalities of income and wealth is based on religious precepts while other approaches represent the result of mundane thinking does not mean that there are no points of similarity between the Islamic and other approaches. When the end objective is the same, there are bound to be some inter-system similarities. As would be noted from the contents of the second chapter of this book, some of the policy prescriptions for the eradication of poverty and reduction in inequalities of income and wealth as deduced from Islamic teachings have their counterpart in other approaches. However, despite these similarities, the Islamic approach has an individuality of its own and is part of a self-contained system.

Islam shares with socialism the concern for an equitable distribution of income and wealth. However, it is strongly opposed to some of the policy instruments advocated by socialist philosophy to achieve this objective. The socialist accent on abolition of private property and socialization of the means of production does not harmonize with the primacy accorded to private enterprise in the Islamic system. Islam attaches great importance to personal freedom and preservation of the dignity of individual human beings. This necessitates that means of production be not monopolized by the state and people be free to engage in all permissible economic activities according to their own proclivities and preferences. In recent years, the socialist states themselves have begun to realize the drawbacks of elimination of private property, and significant moves have been made in a number of countries to liberalize their policies in this respect.

Islam and socialism differ not only with regard to ownership and control of the means of production; they are also markedly different in respect of the locus of economic power, the motivational system and social processes for economic coordination. The socialist state enjoys unfettered freedom in fashioning its policies to achieve its set objectives. In Islam, however, the authority exercised by the state is not absolute. Sovereignty, according to Islam, vests in God.[49] The state authority can, therefore, be exercised only within the norms laid down by *sharī'ah*. For this reason, some of the measures that have been adopted in the history of socialism to combat poverty and reduce inequalities of income and wealth fail to find legitimacy in the Islamic framework. Regimentation, for example, resorted to by certain socialist states to end unemployment and the poverty associated with it cannot be made a component of Islamic strategy to combat poverty because Islam is opposed to it. Similarly, the functional distribution of income, which is tightly controlled by the state under a socialist system, is basically determined by market forces under the Islamic system though the state is expected to intervene whenever social justice considerations warrant such an intervention.

The socialist philosophy does not lay much store by the philanthropic instinct in man to help in the eradication of poverty and reduction in income inequalities. Socialism no doubt implies an acceptance of collective responsibility for eradication of poverty and accords a high priority to the relief of social distress and misfortune. However, it relies exclusively on the state machinery to achieve this purpose. Islam, on the other hand, assigns a prominent role to *infāq* (voluntary spending for the welfare of the poor) in improving the pattern of income distribution. Islam employs a sharply focused motivational system, based on values of faith and religion, to create an urge for welfare spending in the more affluent sections of society. Besides helping to tackle the problems of poverty and income distribution, this approach is intended to create a sense of social solidarity while the approach of socialism is purely mechanistic and impersonal.

Social processes for economic coordination are also markedly different in the two systems. The socialist state effects its policies through comprehensive centralized planning and an elaborate bureaucratic machinery though there are some examples of decentralized socialism and there have been many attempts to reform the system to devolve authority and to spread power and responsibility. The commodity mix of production is generally determined by the state authorities and can diverge significantly from consumer preferences. Commodity prices are controlled. Wage differentials in a socialist society are also determined by the state authorities, and hence there is not much need for fiscal and monetary policies to bring about desired changes in the pattern of income distribution. In the Islamic system, on the other hand, production decisions are basically taken not by a central planning authority but in response to consumer demand though 'consumer sovereignty' may be suitably limited if Islamic imperatives so demand. Commodity prices are determined by the supply and demand factors, and the use of price controls is disfavoured except in extraordinary situations. Wage differentials are generally determined by market forces. Market forces are allowed to operate in other factor markets also though the state is expected to intervene if the market outcome results in hardship for poorer sections of the population and runs counter to other socio-economic objectives. Unlike the position in a socialist state, monetary and fiscal policies are expected to play an important role in bringing about the desired changes in the pattern of income distribution in an Islamic economy.

The Islamic approach to eradication of poverty and containment of inequalities of income and wealth within 'acceptable limits'[50] has several features which distinguish it from the approach employed in capitalist economies to tackle these problems. The most distinguishing feature of the Islamic approach to eradication of poverty is the mandatory character of its social security system. The Qur'ān says: 'Take alms of their wealth, wherewith thou mayst purify them and mayst make them grow.'[51] The main features of Islam's social security system, as it took shape in the early Islamic period, have already been outlined in the preceding chapter. Jurists are agreed that, irrespective of the stage of a country's development and its per capita income, the Islamic teachings make it binding on the state to organize a social security system with a view to ensuring that none should remain deprived of the basic necessities of life. There is no such compelling force in the capitalist philosophy of development. The history of capitalism shows that till the first quarter of the present century, even the highly developed countries of the capitalist world did not think of setting up a comprehensive social security system. Even now the general feeling seems to be that this is a luxury which only the very rich countries can afford. The hard fact is that, despite the growing concern for the poor, the majority of countries in the capitalist world still do not have a 'safety net' for the poor.

The social security systems that have been instituted in the highly developed countries during the course of the present century enjoy a lot of popular support at the moment.

However, unlike the Islamic system, they do not possess any religious sanctity and hence the benefits flowing from them to the poorer sections of society cannot be taken for granted. In fact, lobbies exist which favour the termination of the existing social security system.[52] Influential political groups in many developed industrial nations are advocating significant reductions in the scope and size of the welfare state.[53] It is also noteworthy that in many countries with fairly well developed social security systems there is no definite government commitment that everyone in need will have a guaranteed minimum income.[54] As against this, in the Islamic system, every human being is to be guaranteed a minimum level of living, and many jurists are of the view that legal protection should be afforded to the principle of need fulfilment so that any citizen could go to court to secure the implementation of this principle.[55]

Another distinctive feature of Islam's social security system is that it is focused exclusively on eradication of poverty while the social security programmes of advanced capitalist countries are designed for all citizens, regardless of their individual financial position. It is perhaps for this reason that despite the large size of these programmes, poverty has not been eradicated completely in many of these countries. The social security programmes of advanced capitalist countries are generally structured as a system with both welfare and insurance attributes. In many cases, the insurance attribute far outweighs the welfare attribute. Many analysts are of the view that in many advanced capitalist countries, the poor receive relatively minor transfers from society, and very large amounts of money redistributed by government action represent transfers back and forth within the middle income brackets.[56]

A highly distinctive feature of Islam's social security system is that it seeks to eradicate poverty through a multi-pronged approach and does not confine itself to doling out money to the poor for mere subsistence. In fact, the system is highly personalized in nature and can use a variety of devices both to prevent poverty and remove the hardships caused by poverty. The history of the early Islamic period shows that the social security system even paid for marriage expenses in really hard cases and also paid off the debt of persons in a destitute condition. Great emphasis is given to using the social security system to help the unemployed to earn their own living by providing them with capital assets. Studies of the social security programmes of advanced capitalist countries show that the main emphasis in these programmes is on 'unemployment compensation' rather than on helping those involuntarily unemployed to become gainfully employed.[57]

A good part of the social security programmes in advanced capitalist countries is financed by payroll taxes. For most of the beneficiaries it is fundamentally a pension programme with both the employers and the employees contributing toward the financing of the programme. The taxes paid by the working population are used to pay the retirees. In effect what it means is that each generation of workers undertakes to support the eligible non-working population and implicitly expects similar treatment. The nature of Islam's social security system is markedly different. The pension element does not figure in it at all. Nor is it in the nature of a compulsory contributory saving plan for the future. It merely represents a solidarity fund which derives its resources from the more affluent sections of the population and assists those who are poor and needy. The eligibility to benefit from Islam's social security system does not depend on someone having previously contributed toward the finances of the system nor are the benefits received related in any manner to one's prior contribution.

Islam's social security system is intended to help both in preventing poverty and in overcoming poverty. However, it is just one of the elements of the policy framework that Islam employs for dealing with this problem. The several elements of this policy package, discussed in the second chapter of this book, are all intended to help in the eradication of poverty.

Apart from eradication of poverty, securing of distributional equity also ranks high in the social priorities of an Islamic economy. The most distinctive feature of the Islamic approach to containing inequalities of income and wealth within 'acceptable limits' is that while measures having a distributive or redistributive bearing specifically prescribed by *sharī'ah* (divine guidance as given by the Qur'ān and the *Sunnah*) have to be compulsorily implemented, other measures that are taken should not transgress Islamic teachings and should fulfil the requirement of *al-'adl* (justice).[58] It is also noteworthy that to achieve the aim of distributional equity Islam does not rely on the agency of the state alone but seeks to activate man's moral consciousness to act justly with others and help those in need in a spirit of universal brotherhood.

The state is specifically mandated in the Islamic system to institute a special levy known as *zakāh* whose proceeds can only be used for designated purposes.[59] Since the incidence of *zakāh* is on relatively well-off sections of the population and the proceeds have to be spent primarily for the eradication of poverty so long as poverty exists, it serves a redistributive purpose. To the extent it takes the form of an income maintenance scheme, it reduces the income differential between *zakāh* payers and *zakāh* recipients in the short run. To the extent it is disbursed in the form of productive assets, it results in a more durable increase in the income of the poorer sections of the population.

Distribution of the property of the deceased in strict accordance with the inheritance laws stipulated in *sharī'ah* serves to reduce inequalities of income and wealth over time in an Islamic society.[60] The distinctiveness of Islamic inheritance laws lies in the fact that, as compared to inheritance laws and customs prevalent in many other societies, it leads to wider intergenerational dispersal of accumulated wealth.

Islamic teachings strictly prohibit all interest-based transactions. This obviates the possibility of any addition to the wealth of the owners of money capital until the use of this capital results in the creation of additional wealth. Exploitation of the weaker sections of the population by private money lenders, who charge very high rates of interest, cannot be tolerated in an Islamic economy which must make alternative arrangements for meeting the genuine financial requirements of all sections of society in accordance with the Islamic ideal of social justice.

Islam prescribes a distinctive set of family laws which,

among other things, give legal right to certain close relatives to claim maintenance support from those in a position to help.[61] Islamic teachings urge people to voluntarily assist their poor relatives but in case these teachings are neglected, the courts are empowered to enforce reasonable maintenance support.

Islam employs a distinctive approach in regulating the return on various factors of production to promote distributive justice. It denies any return on money capital unless the owner of this capital is prepared to share in the risks of the business to which capital is provided. Profit/loss sharing is favoured as a more equitable system governing factor returns. Islamic teachings emphasize that labour should be ensured a 'just wage' which preserves human dignity. The state is expected to intervene whenever the owner of a factor of production is seen to exploit a weaker party in the production process.

Islamic teachings prescribe fairly detailed guidelines to regulate business practices and entrust the state with the responsibility to ensure that actual practices conform to these guidelines. The aim is to protect the interests of weaker parties and prevent undue gains in any business transaction. In the early Islamic period, a specific institution known as *ḥisbah* was created which, among other things, was responsible for promoting fair business practices.

Islam allows a good deal of flexibility to state authorities in matters which are not specifically mandated by *sharī'ah*. In fact, *sharī'ah* has prescribed only the essential elements of a basic strategy and detailed policy measures have to be evolved by the state authorities in the light of individual country circumstances. The only requirement is that the policies adopted should make a positive contribution to the realization of *maqāṣid* (objectives) without causing any infringement of *sharī'ah* principles. The main elements of the policy framework for containing inequalities of income and wealth within 'acceptable limits' in present-day world conditions, as deducible from Islamic teachings, have been outlined in the preceding chapter. Quite a few of the policies in this package bear a degree of resemblance to policies which a number of capitalist countries have chosen to follow after the abandonment of the policy of *laissez-faire* under a regime of 'managed capitalism'. Even in these cases, however, there are often differences in the relative emphasis or nuances of the policies. This is particularly noticeable in respect of the role of 'consumer sovereignty' and of monetary, fiscal, and other government policies in determining the allocation of resources.

The composition of output in capitalist countries is generally determined by consumer preferences. In the Islamic system also, consumer preferences are given a wide scope but 'consumer sovereignty' is subject to restraints in the interests of social justice. The capitalist philosophy is that man is free to spend his income in any way he likes[62] and the production structure should respond to consumer demand irrespective of the character of this demand. The resource allocation resulting from this interaction of demand and supply is considered optimal. Islamic teachings, on the other hand, judge the optimality of resource allocation from the viewpoint of *al-'adl* (justice). Jurists have drawn a line of distinction between three types of human needs classified as *ḍarūriyyāt* (necessities), *ḥājiyyāt* (conveniences), and *taḥsīniyyāt* (refinements).[63] They have also indicated that it is the collective responsibility of the society to give precedence to fulfilment of *ḍarūriyyāt* over the other two categories. In an Islamic economy, therefore, the composition of output cannot be left to be determined by market forces alone but would have to be regulated in the interests of social justice.

For the same reason, monetary, fiscal, and other government policies cannot afford to be value neutral in an Islamic economy. In capitalist countries, monetary policy is generally concerned with monetary stability and economic growth, and the goal of distributive justice does not figure prominently in monetary policy objectives. In fact, operations of the banking system appear to have been an important factor in aggravating inequalities of income and wealth in a number of countries. Banks in capitalist countries make financing available mainly to 'creditworthy' businessmen who already own substantial personal wealth and have the ability to offer the collateral required by banks. Banks also practise 'price discrimination' in favour of rich clients with a higher credit rating by charging them lower interest rates.[64] Both these factors tend to aggravate inequalities of income and wealth. On the other hand, monetary policy is expected to play an important role in achieving the egalitarian aims of an Islamic economy.[65]

Fiscal policy in an Islamic economy is constrained by a number of norms prescribed by *sharī'ah*. The state cannot borrow on the basis of interest to cover its budgetary deficit.[66] Islamic teachings emphasize the utmost economy in government expenditure. Many jurists have referred in this connection to the strictures in the Qur'ān on extravagance which apply as much to individuals as to the government. Islamic teachings also emphasize that taxes should be imposed only to finance 'essential expenditure' and the tax burden should be equitably distributed. Though the government in an Islamic economy is not precluded from running a budgetary deficit, it has to so manage its finances that monetary stability is preserved. Economy in government expenditure, equity in the distribution of tax burden, and a policy of 'financial prudence' are accepted as desirable norms of fiscal policy in capitalist economies also but Islamic teachings invest them with greater moral pressure.

Apart from monetary and fiscal policies, the whole orientation of other government policies has an important influence on the pattern of income distribution. It has been observed that despite declared egalitarian objectives, government policies in many capitalist countries have not succeeded in reducing inequalities of income and wealth to any significant extent while in many others inequalities have tended to increase over time. Most capitalist countries remain committed to promote competitive market conditions but in actual practice the economies of many countries are characterized by significant monopoly elements. The weakening of the forces of competition and the emergence of an oligopolistic market structure in many fields of activity has had unfavourable consequences for the pattern of income distribution.[67] The economic history of the U.S.A. and a number of European countries shows that over time the control of industry has become more and more concentrated. This had led some writers to describe the present economic system in these countries as 'monopoly capitalism'.[68] Similarly, in many developing countries, government policies related to trade, tariffs, and industrial and import licensing have had unfavourable effects on the pattern of income distribution. In the Islamic framework, all government policies are expected to be guided by the definite imperative contained in verse 59: 7 of the Qur'ān, that wealth should not be allowed to become 'a commodity between the rich among you'.

It will be seen from the contents of this book that the state is expected to play a very important role in an Islamic economy in eradicating poverty and containing inequalities of income and wealth within acceptable limits. It goes without saying that for the materialization of this expectation it is necessary that state authorities be sincerely guided by Islamic teachings.

Islam does not rely on the agency of the state alone to bring about distributive justice. It seeks to create among its followers a strong sense of social responsibility for the welfare of poorer sections of society. If Islamic teachings are acted upon, distributive justice can be attained while individual liberties are preserved and regimentation is avoided. At one point in this book it was mentioned that some analysts have expressed a great deal of pessimism about the likelihood of eradication of poverty in developing countries as they feel that it is very doubtful that upper income groups will be prepared to make the necessary sacrifice. This reluctance can best be overcome by the infusion of moral values which motivate man to look beyond his own selfish interests. Promotion of the idea of interdependence of utility functions can also help in this respect. Of late it has become increasingly clear that, in a number of important areas, the economy is liable to perform poorly without a minimum of 'benevolence'.[69] A number of works on the role of altruism in an economy have appeared in recent years.[70] Many of these contributions emphasize that once one's perception is aroused, benevolence becomes a rational requirement on action and can be expected to spread throughout the community. Viewed in this perspective, eradication of poverty and securing of greater distributional equity are clearly attainable goals.

Notes and References

1. For an interesting account of hunting and gathering societies, see Gerhard E. Lenski, *Power and Privilege: A Theory of Social Stratification* (McGraw Hill, 1966).

2. *Ibid.*

3. *Ibid.*

4. *Ibid.*

5. *Ibid.*

6. It is reported that as far back as the early Assyrian tablets, records have been found of reformers who sought to alleviate the backbreaking burdens on the peasantry. See Robert L. Heilbroner, *The Making of Economic Society* (Prentice Hall, 1975), p. 31.

7. See Seyyed Mahmood Taleqani, *Islam and Ownership* (Lexington: Mazda Publishers, 1983), pp. 76–7.

8. For details, see Fernand Braudel, *Civilization and Capitalism* (Harper & Row, 1982), Vol. II, pp. 251–5 and 495–7.

9. For details see the chapter on 'The Course of Poverty', in C. T. Morris and I. Adelman, *Comparative Patterns of Economic Development* (The Johns Hopkins University Press, 1988).

10. It is reported that Queen Victoria's *laissez-faire* government let millions of Irish children, women, and men literally starve in the famine of 1848–49. See P. A. Samuelson and William D. Nordhaus, *Economics,* Twelfth Edition (McGraw Hill, 1985), p. 49.

11. It was recognized that pressure of population may depress wages to a subsistence level but this was looked upon as a natural consequence of the 'iron law of wages', a theory associated with the name of a famous economist, David Ricardo.

12. Richard Perlman, *The Economics of Poverty* (McGraw Hill, 1976), pp. 4–5.

13. For details see Karl Polanyi, *The Great Transformation* (New York: Rinehart & Company, 1957), pp. 77–80.

14. For a detailed exposition of Marx's view, see Karl Marx, *Capital: A Critique of Political Economy* (Chicago: Charles H. Kerr and Co., 1906) and Karl Marx and Friedrich Engels, *Manifesto of the Communist Party* (New York: International Publishers Co., 1937).

15. For details see George B. Shaw et al., *The Fabian Essays in Socialism* (Boston: Ball Publishing Co., 1908).

16. See Allan G. Gruchy, *Comparative Economic Systems* (Houghton Mifflin Company, 1977), p. 523.

17. For details see Morris Bornstein (ed.), *Plan and Market, Economic Reform in Eastern Europe* (Yale University Press, 1973).

18. For some details see John E. Elliott, *Comparative Economic Systems* (Belmont: Wadsworth Publishing Company, 1985), pp. 408–29.

19. See Keith Griffin, *Alternative Strategies for Economic Development* (London: Macmillan, 1989), pp. 218–19.

20. *Ibid.*

21. See Allan G. Gruchy, *Comparative Economic Systems, op. cit.*, p. 627.

22. *Ibid.*

23. See Keith Griffin, *Alternative Strategies for Economic Development, op. cit.*, pp. 194–225.

24. *Ibid.*

25. Martin C. Schnitzer, *Comparative Economic Systems* (Cincinnati: South-Western Publishing Group, 1987), pp. 153–4.

26. For details of the social security programmes, see the U.S. Department of Health, Education, and Welfare, *Social Security Programs Throughout the World* (Washington: U.S. Government Printing Office, 1986).

27. The countries included in the study are Australia, Belgium, Great Britain, and Norway. Wilfred Beckerman, *Poverty and the Impact of Income Maintenance Programmes in Four Developed Countries* (Geneva: International Labour Organization, 1979).

28. For more details see Allan G. Gruchy, *Comparative Economic Systems, op. cit.*, pp. 374–5.

29. See, for example, William N. Loucks, *Comparative Economic Systems* (Harper & Row, 1965), p. 51.

30. See Nanak C. Kakwani, *Income Inequality and Poverty* (Oxford University Press, 1980), pp. 397–8.

31. *Ibid.*

32. See Keith Griffin and A. R. Khan, 'Poverty in the Third World: Ugly Facts and Fancy Models', *World Development,* March 1978.

33. D. Morawetz, 'Twenty Five Years of Economic Development', *Finance and Development,* September 1977, p. 10.

34. I. Adelman and C. T. Morris, *Economic Growth and Social Equity in Developing Countries* (Stanford University Press, 1973).

35. IBRD, *World Development Report, 1985* (New York: Oxford University Press, 1985), pp. 228–9.

36. See Nanak C. Kakwani, *Income Inequality and Poverty, op. cit.*, pp. 390–8.

37. A number of research studies have shown that there is no strong pattern relating changes in the distribution of income to the rate of growth of GNP. In both high-growth and low-growth countries there are some which have experienced improvement and others that have experienced deterioration in relative equality. For details and country examples, see Hollis Chenery, et al., *Redistribution with Growth* (Oxford University Press, 1974), pp. 11–16.

38. For the most famous enunciation of this hypothesis see Simon Kuznets, 'Economic Growth and Income Inequality', *American Economic Review,* March 1955.

39. See, in this connection, S. Anand and S. Kanbur, 'Inequality and Development: A Reconsideration', in Hans-Peter Nissen (ed.), *Towards Income Distribution Policies: From Income Distribution Research to Income Distribution Policy in LDCs* (Tilburg: Development Research Institute, 1984).

40. See G. F. Papanek, 'Economic Growth, Income Distribution and the Political Process in Less Developed Countries', in Zvi Griliches, et al. (eds.), *Income Distribution and Economic Inequality* (John Wiley & Sons, 1978).

41. See Hollis Chenery, et al., *Redistribution with Growth, op. cit.*

42. See International Labour Organization, *Employment, Growth and Basic Needs* (Geneva, 1976)

43. Two countries, Taiwan and South Korea, have adopted more determined income redistributive policies and have achieved greater success in alleviation of poverty and reduction in income inequalities.

44. ILO, *Employment, Growth and Basic Needs, op. cit.*

45. *Ibid.*

46. See, for example, Keith Griffin, *Alternative Strategies for Economic Development, op. cit.*, p. 169.

47. See the chapter on 'The Political Framework', in Hollis Chenery, et al., *Redistribution with Growth, op. cit.*, especially pp. 71–2.

48. See the Development Committee document *Strengthening Efforts to Reduce Poverty* (Washington, 1989), pp. 18–19.

49. 'Sovereignty is for none but God' (Qur'ān, 12: 40).

50. For a discussion of the factors having a bearing on the determination of the 'acceptable limits' of inequalities of income and wealth in an Islamic economy see pp. 19–21 of this book.

51. Qur'ān, 9: 103.

52. For an articulation of such a view, see Helen P. Rogers, *Social Security: An Idea Whose Time Has Passed* (Wellington Publications, 1986).

53. See Henry Aaron, 'Cutting Back the Social Welfare State', in Sijbren Cnossen (ed.), *Comparative Tax Studies: Essays in Honour of Richard Goode* (Amsterdam: North-Holland Publishing Company, 1983).

54. See, in this connection, the statement of the Ad Hoc Committee on Triple Revolution, in E. C. Budd (ed.), *Inequality and Poverty* (New York: W. W. Norton & Co., 1967).

55. See Muhammad Nejatullah Siddiqi, 'The Guarantee of a Minimum Level of Living in an Islamic State', in Munawar Iqbal (ed.), *Distributive Justice and Need Fulfilment in an Islamic Economy* (Islamabad: International Institute of Islamic Economics; Leicester: The Islamic Foundation, 1988), pp. 251–86.

56. See Gordon Tullock, 'The Charity of the Uncharitable', in The Institute of Economic Affairs, *The Economics of Charity* (The Gresham Press, 1973), p. 26.

57. See, for example, Oscar Ornati, *Poverty Amid Affluence: A Report on a Research Project* (New York: The Twentieth Century Fund, 1966), pp. 115–19.

58. 'Say: My Lord enjoineth justice' (Qur'ān, 7: 29).

59. The details of this levy can be found on pp. 48–52 of this book.

60. For a description of the inheritance laws of Islam see pp. 34–6 of this book.

61. For details see p. 47 of this book.

62. Even in capitalist societies some restraints are put on 'consumer sovereignty' to prevent social damage like prohibition on production and consumption of drugs. Consumer sovereignty is also restricted when the import of certain goods may be banned due to shortage of foreign exchange. However, such restrictions are not related to considerations of social justice.

63. For an elaboration of this concept and reference to juristic literature on the subject see p. 19 of this book.

64. Such behaviour on the part of banks is regarded as perfectly logical and natural in a capitalist framework. Mishan, for example, says: 'Given that differences in wealth are substantial, it would be irrational for the lender to be willing to lend as much to the impecunious as to the richer members of the society, or to lend the same amounts on the same terms to each.' E. S. Mishan, *Cost Benefit Analysis* (New York: Praeger, 1971), p. 205.

65. See, in this connection, M. U. Chapra, *Towards a Just Monetary System* (Leicester: The Islamic Foundation, 1985), especially pp. 173–4 and 200–2.

66. For a fuller treatment of this subject, see Ziauddin Ahmad, 'Public Finance in Islam', IMF Working Paper (WP/89/68), pp. 15–17.

67. See Tibor Scitovsky, *Welfare and Competition* (Richard D. Irwin Inc., 1951), pp. 439–43.

68. See Paul A. Baran and Paul M. Sweezy, *Monopoly Capital* (New York: Monthly Review Press, 1966) and Keith Cowling, *Monopoly Capitalism* (John Wiley & Sons, 1982).

69. See, in this connection, the essay on 'Morality and the Social Sciences: A Durable Tension', in Albert O. Hirschman, *Essays in Trespassing: Economics to Politics and Beyond* (Cambridge University Press, 1981).

70. See, for example, Kenneth E. Boulding, *The Economy of Love and Fear: A Preface to Grants Economics* (Belmont: Wadsworth Publishing Company, 1973); David Collard, *Altruism and Economy: A Study in Non-Selfish Economics* (Oxford University Press, 1978); Edmund S. Phelps (ed.), *Altruism, Morality and Economic Theory* (New York: Russell Sage Foundation, 1975).

CHAPTER 4

Summary and Conclusions

Distributive justice is one of the most important components of the Islamic vision of a just socio-economic order. Islam stands for complete eradication of absolute poverty and organization of economic life in a manner that the basic needs of all human beings are met. It does not call for the obliteration of all inequalities of income and wealth but cautions against glaring inequalities. To ensure fulfilment of the basic needs of all, Islam enunciates the principle of the poor having a 'right' in the income and wealth of the well-off members of the society. Islamic laws and economic teachings in the sphere of production, consumption, exchange, and distribution are all designed to secure distributive justice and an equitable pattern of income and wealth distribution.

This book sets out the main elements of a policy framework for the eradication of poverty and achievement of an equitable distribution of income and wealth which can be discerned and deduced from Islamic teachings. First of all, Islam encourages productive effort. It exhorts all able-bodied persons to earn their living and desist from seeking assistance from others except in the event of desperate need. By way of development strategy, the general message of Islam is for a dynamic change over time through technological advancement. Besides overall rate of growth, Islam is greatly concerned with the mechanics of growth and the pattern of growth. It envisages productive activity to be undertaken primarily on the basis of private enterprise but gives the state the right to influence and regulate the working of the private sector to achieve the objectives of the Islamic system. Islam intends that growth should be broad-based, and the generation of maximum feasible employment opportunities has the strongest claim to be accorded top priority in an Islamically-oriented growth strategy.

Islamic teachings prescribe a comprehensive code of business ethics which seeks to eliminate all exploitative practices. The main aim of regulating business practices is to prevent undue enrichment of some at the expense of the many and thereby to curb inequalities of income and wealth.

Islam is strongly opposed to social stratification and emphasizes equality of opportunity. Property rights in Islam carry certain obligations. If these obligations are not carried out, the state can intervene in the interests of social justice. Distribution of the property of the deceased has to take place in strict accordance with Islamic inheritance laws which lead to wide intergenerational dispersal of accumulated wealth.

Islamic teachings have an important bearing on factor shares and functional distribution of income which in turn have implications for size distribution of personal income. Money capital is denied entitlement to any return if it is just lent to someone for a specified period of time. This means that no one can earn any income in an Islamic economy by charging interest. Profit/loss sharing is favoured as an equitable system governing factor returns. Islamic teachings emphasize that labour should be ensured a 'just wage' which preserves human dignity. The state is expected to intervene whenever the owner of a factor of production is seen to exploit a weaker party in the production process.

Islam greatly encourages voluntary spending for the welfare of the poor. Feeding the hungry is stressed again and again, so much so that repelling the orphan and neglect of the feeding of the destitute are equated to denial of the religion itself. The amount of wealth that should be spent for the welfare of the poor has not been specified in precise quantitative terms. However, there is a general indication in one of the verses in the Qur'ān that any surplus above one's genuine needs should be so spent. The family laws of Islam give legal right to certain close relatives to claim maintenance support from those in a position to help. Islamic teachings urge people to voluntarily assist their poor relatives but in case these teachings are neglected, the courts are empowered to enforce reasonable maintenance support.

Fiscal and monetary policies are expected to play a very important role in eradicating poverty and curbing inequalities of income and wealth in an Islamic economy. Tax policies should be judicious and desist from aggravating inequalities of income and wealth. Eradication of poverty and removal of the hardships of the poorer sections of the population should figure prominently in the priorities of public expenditure. To help achieve Islamic socio-economic objectives, monetary policy would need to be used to so regulate the use of the financial resources of the banking system that it helps significantly in reducing inequalities of income and wealth and achieving a product mix that is in line with Islamic priorities. Both fiscal and monetary policies are expected to promote monetary stability which, among other things, safeguards the interests of the poor.

Islamic teachings assign to the state the ultimate responsibility of ensuring at least a basic minimum standard of living for all citizens. For this purpose it is incumbent on the state to establish a social security system in which the religiously ordained levy of *zakāh* (poor due) plays a central role. The bulk of the financing needed for Islam's social security system is expected to come from *zakāh* proceeds. However, in case proceeds from *zakāh* do not suffice for the purpose, these have to be supplemented from the general budgetary resources to the extent considered necessary.

This study also seeks to bring out the distinctiveness of the Islamic approach to issues of poverty and income distribution compared to certain other systemic approaches. It surveys the attitudes and policies toward poverty and inequalities of income and wealth from ancient times to modern times, and takes particular note of similarities and dissimilarities between the Islamic approach and the approaches under the two presently dominant systems of managed capitalism and socialism. It is seen that though Islam shares with socialism the concern for an equitable distribution of income and wealth, it is strongly opposed to some of the policy instruments advocated by socialist philosophy to achieve this objective. Islam and socialism differ not only with regard to ownership and control of the means of production; they are also markedly different in respect of locus of economic power, the motivational system, and social processes for economic co-ordination.

As compared to managed capitalism, the most distinguishing feature of the Islamic approach to eradication of poverty is the mandatory character of its social security system. The history of capitalism shows that until the first quarter of the present century, even the highly developed countries of the capitalist world did not think of setting up a comprehensive social security system. Even now the general feeling seems to be that this is a luxury which only the very rich countries can afford. The hard fact is that, despite the growing concern for the poor, the majority of countries in the capitalist world still do not have a 'safety net' for the poor. As against this, Islamic teachings make it binding on the state to organize a social security system to ensure fulfilment of the basic needs of all irrespective of the stage of a country's development and its per capita income. The study also notes the main points of distinction between Islam's social security system and the social security systems of the present-day economically advanced countries.

Quite a few policies advocated by Islam in the interests of distributional equity bear a degree of resemblance to policies which a number of capitalist countries have chosen to follow after the abandonment of the policy of *laissez-faire*. Even in these cases, however, there are often differences in the relative emphasis or nuances of policies. This is particularly noticeable in respect of the role of 'consumer sovereignty' and of monetary, fiscal, and other government policies in determining the allocation of resources.

Glossary

Al-'Adl	Justice
Al-'afw	Beyond one's needs
Fuqarā' (sing. *Faqīr*)	The poor
Ḥisbah	An institution for encouraging Islamic norms of behaviour and checking unlawful practices
'Ibādah	Worship
Iḥsān	Benevolence
Ijmā'	Consensus of the jurists
Ijtihād	A jurist's use of his reasoning to find solutions to new problems not explicitly covered in the Qur'ān and the *Sunnah* keeping in full view the intent and spirit of Islam
Infāq	Voluntary spending for the welfare of the poor/cause of Islam
Khums	A levy of twenty per cent
Manīḥah	Granting of usufruct of a productive asset to a needy person for a specific period
Maqāṣid	Objectives
Masākīn (sing. *Miskīn*)	The needy
Al-maṣlaḥah al-'āmmah	General good
Muḍārabah	A profit and loss sharing contract in which one party provides capital and the other party manages the enterprise. In case of loss the

	provider of capital bears the financial loss while the worker loses his labour. In case of profit both parties share it in agreed proportions
Mushārakah	Equity participation agreement
Muzāra'ah	Share-cropping contract
Nafaqāt (sing. *Nafaqah*)	Obligatory maintenance by relatives
Niṣāb	The minimum quantity or amount of an asset which makes it liable to *zakāh*
Nuṣūṣ (sing. *Naṣṣ*)	Conclusive injunctions of the Qur'ān and the *Sunnah* from which no departure is allowed in any age
Qiyās	Analogical deduction
Qur'ān	The Book consisting of revelations made by God to the Prophet Muḥammad
Ṣadaqah	Charity/voluntary contribution for a good cause
Sharī'ah	Code of conduct as laid down in the Qur'ān and the *Sunnah*
Sunnah	The way of the Prophet comprising of what he did or said or tacitly approved
'Ushr	*Zakāh* on agricultural produce
Waqf	Endowment for general or specific purposes under Islamic law
Wasq	A measure equivalent to 190 kg.
Zakāh	Poor due; poor tax on the wealth of well-to-do Muslims in accordance with the provisions of *Sharī'ah*

Select Bibliography*

Aaron, Henry, 'Cutting Back the Social Welfare State', in Sijbren Cnossen (ed.), *Comparative Tax Studies: Essays in Honour of Richard Goode* (North-Holland Publishing Company, 1983).

al-'Abbādī, 'Abd al-Salām, *Al-Milkiyyah fī al-Sharī'ah al-Islāmiyyah* (Ammān: Maktabat al-Aqṣā, A.H. 1394).

Abū 'Ubaid, *Kitāb al-Amwāl* (Cairo: Dār al-Fikr, A.H. 1395).

Abū Ya'lā, *Al-Aḥkām al-Sulṭānīyah* (Beirut: Dār al-Fikr).

Abū Yūsuf, *Kitāb al-Kharāj* (Cairo: Maṭba'a Salafiyah, A.H. 1392).

Abū Zahrah, *Tanẓīm al-Islām li'l Mujtama'* (Cairo: Dār al-Fikr al-'Arabī, 1975).

Adelman, Irma and C. T. Morris, *Economic Growth and Social Equity in Developing Countries* (Stanford University Press, 1973).

al-Ahl, 'Abd al-'Azīz Sayyid, *al-Khalīfah az-Zāhid 'Umar ibn 'Abd al-Azīz* (Beirut: Dār al-'Ilm li'l Mala'yīn, 1973).

Ahmad, Khurshid (ed.), *Islam: Its Meaning and Message* (Leicester: The Islamic Foundation, 1975).

——, (ed.), *Studies in Islamic Economics* (Leicester: The Islamic Foundation, 1980).

Ahmad, Ziauddin, 'Public Finance in Islam', IMF Working Paper (WP/89/68).

——, et al. (eds.), *Fiscal Policy and Resource Allocation in Islam* (Islamabad: Institute of Policy Studies and International Centre for Research in Islamic Economics, 1983).

——, et al. (eds.), *Money and Banking in Islam* (Islamabad: Institute of Policy Studies and International Centre for Research in Islamic Economics, 1983).

Anand S. and S. Kanbur, 'Inequality and Development: A Reconsideration', in Hans-Peter Nissen (ed.), *Towards Income Distribution Policies: From Income Distribution Re-*

*Apart from books and articles referred to in this study, this bibliography lists other published material which may be of interest to those who want to do further readings on the subject matter of this book and its related themes.

search to Income Distribution Policy in LDCs (Tilburg: Development Research Institute, 1984).
Ariff, M. (ed.), *Monetary and Fiscal Economics of Islam* (Jeddah: International Centre for Research in Islamic Economics, 1978).
'Audah, 'Abd al-Qādir, *al-Māl wa'l-ḥukm fi'l-Islām* (Jeddah: ad-Dār as-Sa'ūdiyyah bin-Nashr, 1969).
al-Balādhurī, *Futūḥ al-Buldān* (Beirut: Dār al-Kutub al-'Ilmīyah, 1978).
Baran, Paul A. and Paul M. Sweezy, *Monopoly Capital* (New York: Monthly Review Press, 1966).
Bayyoumi, Z. M., *Al-Māliyah Al-'Āmmah Al-Islāmīyah* (Cairo: Dār al-Naḥḍah al-'Arabīyah).
Beckerman, W., *Poverty and the Impact of Income Maintenance Programmes in Four Developed Countries* (Geneva: International Labour Organization, 1979).
Bornstein, Morris (ed.), *Plan and Market, Economic Reform in Eastern Europe* (Yale University Press, 1973).
Boulding, Kenneth E., *The Economy of Love and Fear: A Preface to Grants Economics* (Belmont: Wadsworth Publishing Company, 1973).
Braudel, Fernand, *Civilization and Capitalism,* Volume II (New York: Harper & Row, 1982).
Bronfenbrenner, M., *Income Distribution Theory* (Macmillan, 1971).
Budd, E. C. (ed.), *Inequality and Poverty* (New York: W. W. Norton & Co., 1967).
al-Bukhārī, *al-Adab al-Mufrad* (Cairo: Quṣayy Muḥibb al-Dīn al-Khaṭīb, A.H. 1379).
——, *al-Jāmi' al-Ṣaḥīḥ* (Maktabah al-Riyāḍ al-Ḥadīthah, 1981).
Chapra, M. U., *Towards a Just Monetary System* (Leicester: The Islamic Foundation, 1985).
Chenery, Hollis, et al., *Redistribution with Growth* (Oxford University Press, 1974).
Collard, David, *Altruism and Economy: A Study in Non-Selfish Economics* (Oxford University Press, 1978).
Cowling, Keith, *Monopoly Capitalism* (John Wiley & Sons, 1982).
Dalton, George, *Economic Systems and Society* (Penguin Books Inc., 1974).
Development Committee, *Strengthening Efforts to Reduce Poverty* (Washington, 1989).
Elliott, J. E., *Comparative Economic Systems* (Belmont: Wadsworth Publishing Company, 1985).

Friedman, Milton, *Capitalism and Freedom* (University of Chicago Press, 1962).

al-Ghazālī, *Kitāb al-Iqtiṣād fī al-I'tiqād* (Beirut: Dār al-Amānah).

Goldstein, Richard and S. M. Sachs, *Applied Poverty Research* (Rowman & Allanheld, 1983).

Gordon, M. S., *The Economics of Welfare Policies* (New York: Columbia University Press, 1963).

Gordon, Scott, *Welfare, Justice and Freedom* (New York: Columbia University Press, 1980).

Griffin, Keith, *Alternative Strategies for Economic Development* (London: Macmillan, 1989).

——, *International Inequality and National Poverty* (London: Macmillan, 1978).

Griffin, Keith and A. R. Khan, 'Poverty in the Third World: Ugly Facts and Fancy Models', *World Developments,* March 1978.

Griliches, Zvi, et al. (eds.), *Income Distribution and Economic Inequality* (John Wiley & Sons, 1978).

Gruchy, Allan, *Comparative Economic Systems* (Houghton Mifflin Company, 1977).

Gustafsson, B. A. and N. A. Klevmarken, *The Political Economy of Social Security* (Amsterdam: North-Holland Publishing Company, 1989).

al-Ḥākim, *Al-Mustadrak 'alā Aṣ-Ṣaḥīḥayn* (Aleppo, Maktab Al-Maṭbū'āt Al-Islāmīyah, n.d.).

Hasanuz Zaman, S. M., *Economic Functions of an Islamic State* (Leicester: The Islamic Foundation, 1991).

Haykal, M. H., *The Life of Muhammad* (North American Trust Publications, 1976).

Heilbroner, R. L., *The Making of Economic Society* (Prentice Hall, 1975).

Hirschman, Albert O., 'Morality and the Social Sciences: A Durable Tension', in his *Essays in Trespassing: Economics to Politics and Beyond* (Cambridge University Press, 1981).

Huwaydī, A., *Mabādi al-Māliyah al-'Āmmah fī al-Sharī'ah al-Islāmīyah* (Cairo: Dār al-Fikr al-'Arabī).

Ibn 'Ābidīn, *Hāshiyah Radd al-Muḥtār* (Cairo: Matba'ah Haimaniyah).

Ibn Anas, Mālik, *al-Muwaṭṭa'* (Beirut: Dār al-Nafais, 1973).

Ibn Ḥanbal, Aḥmad, *Musnad al-Imām Aḥmad* (Beirut: Dār Ṣādir, 1969).

Ibn Hazm, *Kitāb al-Muḥallā* (Cairo: Al-Munīrīyah, A.H. 1347).

Ibn Mājah, *Sunan Ibn Mājah* (Riyadh: Sharikah at-Ṭibā'ah al-'Arabīyah as-Sa'ūdīyah, 1984).

Ibn Qayyim, *I'lām al-Muwaqqi'īn* (Cairo: Maktabah al-Sa'ādah, 1955).
Ibn Sa'd, Muḥammad, *al-Ṭabaqāt al-Kubrā* (Beirut: Dār Ṣādir li'l Ṭibā'ah wa al-Nashr, 1968).
Ibn Taimīyah, *Al-Ḥisbah fī al-Islām* (Cairo: Dār al-Sha'b, 1976).
——, *Majmū' Fatāwā Shaikh al-Islām Aḥmad ibn Taimīyah* (Riyadh: Al-Riyad Press, 1971).
——, *al-Siyāsah al-Shar'īyah fī Aḥwāl al-Rā'ī wa'l Ra'īyah* (Cairo: Dār al-Kutub al-'Arabīyah, 1971).
Ibrāhīm, Aḥmad Ibn Ibrāhīm, *Niẓām al-Nafaqāt fī al-Sharī'ah al-Islāmīyah* (Cairo: al-Maṭba'ah al-Salafīyah, A.H. 1349).
International Bank for Reconstruction and Development, *World Development Report, 1985* (Oxford University Press, 1985).
International Labour Organization, *The Cost of Social Security, Twelfth International Inquiry* (Geneva, 1988).
——, *Employment, Growth and Basic Needs* (Geneva, 1976).
Iqbal, Javid, 'Human Rights in Islam', in *Islamic Law and Social and Economic Development* (Islamabad: Idarah Saqafat-e-Pakistan, n.d.).
Iqbal, Munawar (ed.), *Distributive Justice and Need Fulfilment in an Islamic Economy* (Leicester: The Islamic Foundation, 1988).
Iṣlāḥī, A. A., *Economic Concepts of Ibn Taimīyah* (Leicester: The Islamic Foundation, 1988).
Al-Jazīrī, 'Abd al-Raḥmān, *Kitāb al-fiqh 'alā al-madhāhib al-Arba'ah* (Cairo: Al-Maktabah al-tijāriyyah al-kubrā, 1969).
Kakwani, Nanak C., *Income Inequality and Poverty* (Oxford University Press, 1980).
Khan, M. S. and A. Mirakhor, 'Reordering the Economic System: A Perspective from the Fundamental Sources of Islam' (mimeo).
Kuznets, Simon, 'Economic Growth and Income Inequality', *American Economic Review,* March 1955.
Lange, Oskar, 'On the Economic Theory of Socialism', *Review of Economic Studies,* October 1936 and February 1937.
Lenski, Gerhard E., *Power and Privilege: A Theory of Social Stratification* (McGraw Hill, 1966).
Loucks, W. N., *Comparative Economic Systems* (Harper & Row, 1965).
al-Marghīnānī, *al-Hidāyah* (Cairo: Isa al-Bābī al-Ḥalabī & Co.).
Marx, Karl, *Capital: A Critique of Political Economy* (Chicago: Charles H. Kerr and Co., 1906).
Marx, Karl and Friedrich Engels, *Manifesto of the Communist Party* (New York: International Publishers Co., 1937).

al-Māwardī, *Al-Aḥkām al-Sulṭānīyah* (Cairo: Maṭba'at al-waṭan, A.H. 1398).
——, *Kitāb Adab al-Dunyā wal-Dīn* (Beirut: Dār Iḥyā' al-Turāth al-'Arabī).
Mirakhor, A., 'The Economic System in an Islamic Society', *Middle East Insight,* Vol. 5, No. 3, 1987.
Mishan, E. S., *Cost Benefit Analysis* (New York: Praeger, 1971).
Morawetz, D., 'Twenty Five Years of Economic Development', *Finance and Development,* September 1977.
Morris, C. T. and Irma Adelman, *Comparative Patterns of Economic Development* (The Johns Hopkins University Press, 1988).
al-Mundhirī, *Mukhtaṣar Ṣaḥīḥ Muslim* (Kuwait: al-Dār al-Kuwaitiyah liṭṭibā'ah wan Nashr Wa'l-Tawzī', 1969).
Munnell, A. H., *The Future of Social Security* (Washington: The Brookings Institution, 1977).
al-Nawawī, *Minhāj al-Ṭālibīn wa 'Umdat al-Muftiyīn* (Cairo: Dār Iḥyā' al-Kutub al-'Arabiyyah).
Nove, Alec, *Socialism, Economics and Development* (London: Allen & Unwin, 1986).
Ornati, Oscar, *Poverty Amid Affluence: A Report on a Research Project* (New York: The Twentieth Century Fund, 1966).
Papanek, G. F., 'Economic Growth, Income Distribution and the Political Process in Less Developed Countries', in Zvi Griliches et al. (eds.), *Income Distribution and Economic Inequality* (John Wiley & Sons, 1978).
Pechman, J. A. et al., *Social Security: Perspectives for Reform* (Washington: The Brookings Institution, 1968).
Perlman, Richard, *The Economics of Poverty* (McGraw Hill, 1976).
Phelps, Edmund S. (ed.), *Altruism, Morality and Economic Theory* (New York: Russell Sage Foundation, 1975).
Polanyi, Karl, *The Great Transformation* (New York: Rinehart & Company, 1957).
al-Qarḍāwī, Y., *Fiqh al-Zakāh* (Beirut: Mu'assasat al-Risālah, 1973).
al-Qurṭubī, *al-Jāmi' li-aḥkām al-Qur'ān* (Beirut: Dār al-Fikr, 1987).
Quṭb, Muḥammad, *Al-Insān Bayn al-Māddiyyah wa al-Islām* (Cairo: 'Īsā al-Bābī al-Ḥalabī, 1965).
Quṭb, Sayyid, *Al-'Adālah al-Ijtimā'iyah fī al-Islām,* translated by J. B. Hardie: *Social Justice in Islam* (Washington, 1953).
Ramaḍan, S., *Islamic Law: Its Scope and Equity* (London: Macmillan, 1961).

Rogers, Helen P., *Social Security: An Idea Whose Time Has Passed* (Wellington Publications, 1986).

al-Ṣadr, M. B., *Iqtiṣādunā* (Beirut: Dār al-Ta'arīf lil maṭbū'āt, 1982).

Samuelson, Paul A. and W. D. Nordhaus, *Economics,* Twelfth Edition (McGraw Hill, 1985).

al-Sarakhsī, *Kitāb al-Mabsūṭ* (Cairo: Maṭba'at al-Sa'ādah, A.H. 1324).

Schnitzer, M. C., *Comparative Economic Systems* (Cincinnati: South-Western Publishing Group, 1987).

Scitovsky, Tibor, *Welfare and Competition* (Richard D. Irwin Inc., 1951).

al-Shāṭibī, *al-Muwāfaqāt fī Uṣūl al-Sharī'ah* (Cairo: Maktabah al-Tijārīyah al-Kubrā, n.d.).

Shaw, George B. et al., *The Fabian Essays in Socialism* (Boston: Ball Publishing Co., 1908).

Shonfield, A., *Modern Capitalism* (Oxford University Press, 1965).

Sibā'ī, Muṣṭafā, *Min Rawā'i' Ḥaḍāratinā* (Beirut: Dār al-Qur'ān al-Karīm, 1980).

Siddiqi, M. N., 'The Guarantee of a Minimum Level of Living in an Islamic State', in M. Iqbal (ed.), *Distributive Justice and Need Fulfilment in an Islamic Economy* (Islamabad: International Institute of Islamic Economics; Leicester: The Islamic Foundation, 1988).

as-Suyūṭi, J., *History of the Caliphs,* English translation by H. S. Jarret (Amsterdam: Oriental Press).

al-Tabrīzī, *Mishkāt al-Maṣābīḥ* (Damascus: al-Maktab al-Islāmī, ed. M. Nāṣir al-Dīn al-Albānī, A.H. 1381).

Ṭaleqāni, Seyyed Maḥmood, *Islam and Ownership* (Lexington: Mazda Publishers, 1983).

Thurow, Lester C., *Generating Inequality* (New York: Basic Books, 1975).

Tinbergen, J., *Income Differences: Recent Research* (Amsterdam: North-Holland Publishing Company, 1975).

al-Tirmidhī, *al-Jāmi' aṣ-Ṣaḥīḥ* (Beirut: Dār al-Fikr, 1974).

Tullock, Gordon, 'The Charity of the Uncharitable', in The Institute of Economic Affairs, *The Economics of Charity* (The Gresham Press, 1973).

Tyser, C. R. et al., (English translation of) *The Mejelle* (Lahore: Punjab Eductional Press, 1967).

U.S. Department of Health, Education and Welfare, *Social Security Programs throughout the World* (Washington: U.S. Government Printing Office, 1986).

U.S. House of Representatives, Select Committee on Hunger, *Report on Banking for the Poor: Alleviating Poverty through Credit Assistance to the Poorest Micro-Entrepreneurs in Developing Countries* (Washington: U.S. Government Printing Office, May 1986).

Wiles, Peter J. D., *Distribution of Income: East and West* (Amsterdam: North-Holland Publishing Company, 1974).

Yaḥyā ibn Ādam, *Kitāb al-Kharāj* (Cairo: Maktabah Salafiyah).

Zarqa, M. A., 'Islamic Distributive Schemes', in M. Iqbal (ed.), *Distributive Justice and Need Fulfilment in an Islamic Economy* (Islamabad: International Institute of Islamic Economics; Leicester: The Islamic Foundation, 1988).

Index

Abū Bakr, 18
Adam, 16
'Adl, 21, 84, 86
'Adl wa'l-iḥsān, 37
Adulteration, 31
Africa, 64, 75, 77
'Afw, 42
Agrarian societies, 62–3
Agriculture, 41, 49, 51, 63–4, 70
Allah/God, 5–6, 15–16, 18–19, 26, 28, 32, 35, 37, 42, 48, 79
'Aql, 19
Arabia, 63
Asia, 62, 64, 74
Asset(s), 27–8, 34, 44, 50, 62, 83; productive, 27–8, 34, 84

Banking system, 32, 46, 86, 97
Bank(s), 32, 46, 69; deposits, 50
Bismarck, 72
Budget, 9, 45, 52, 97; deficit, 87
Buildings, 43, 50
Business(es), 30–1, 39, 46, 62, 85; ethics, 30; practices, 30–1, 85

Capital, 9, 37–9, 41, 53, 76
Capitalism, 7, 9, 64, 66–8, 72–3, 81–2, 86, 88, 97–8
Charity, 18, 27, 43
China, 70–1, 74
Christianity, 63
Collectivization, 70
Colonialism, 73
Commerce, 62
Commodity, 81; markets, 29, 64
Communism, 66
Compensation, 34
Consumer(s), 31, 71, 80, 86, 98
Council for Islamic Ideology, 8
Cuba, 71

Ḍarūriyyāt, 19, 86
Day of Judgement, 6
Debt(s), 35–6, 48, 50, 53
Deflation, 47
Depreciation, 41
Deprivation, 5, 17
Destitution, 7, 42, 48, 53, 96
Dīn, 19
Dinārs, 50
Dirhams, 44, 50
Discrimination, 31
Distribution, 95; state control of, 61

Education, 9, 29, 32, 45, 69, 76
Egalitarian(ism), 69, 72–3, 87; bias, 63; objectives, 87; society, 13
Employees, 41–2, 83
Employers, 41, 83
Employment, 10, 29, 46–7, 66, 68, 95; opportunities, 28–9, 44–5
Enclosures movement, 63
England, 63, 65
Entrepreneur(s), 9, 38–9, 46
Europe, 62–4, 70–1, 87
Exchange, 95
Exploitation, 7, 27, 66, 84–5; practices, 30, 96

Factor markets, 64
Factor shares, 36, 96
Faqr, 6
Feudalism, 63
Fiqh, 11
Fiscal: policies, 29, 44, 46–7, 80–1, 86–7, 97–8; system, 44

France, 73
Free market, 64, 67
Fuqarā', 48

Germany, 72–3
God, *see* Allah
Great Depression, 67–8, 72
Gross Domestic Product, 29, 52, 64
Gross National Product, 61, 74, 77
Growth, 27, 75–6, 86; mechanics of, 27, 95; pattern of, 27–8, 95; rate of, 27, 71, 95; strategy, 29, 46, 96

Ḥājiyyāt, 19, 86
Ḥaqq, 17
Health, 9, 29, 45, 76; insurance, 72
Heir(s), 34–6
Hereafter, 11, 17, 30, 42, 47–8
Ḥisbah, 9, 30, 40, 85
Hoarding, 31
Horticulture, 62
Hungary, 70

'Ibādah, 26, 51
Iḥsān, 21, 42
Ijmā', 50
Ijtihād, 25, 49
Imports, 32
Income, 53, 61–3, 66–9, 82; distribution of, 9, 11, 13, 16, 19–20, 64, 66, 70–1, 74, 76, 80–1, 88, 96–7; national, 73; private, 66, 73
Income and wealth, 9, 17, 37; differentials, 20; distribution of, 11, 16, 19–21, 25, 32–4, 36, 39, 61, 69, 75–7, 87; inequalities of, 11, 13, 19–21, 27–8, 30, 32, 34, 36, 44–6, 62, 66–71, 73–5, 78–9, 81, 83–5, 87–8, 95–7
Industrial Revolution, 64
Infāq, 17, 42–3, 80
Inflation, 47
Inheritance, 35–6; laws, 34, 84
Interest, 37–40, 84, 87, 96
International Labour Organization (ILO), 76–7
International Monetary Fund (IMF), 77
Investment, 32, 45, 76
Islam, *passim*
Iṭ'ām, 42

Judaism, 63

Kampuchea, 71
Keynes, 67
Khums, 51
Kufr, 6

Land, 37, 40–1, 43, 50, 62
Landlord, 40
Latin America, 75
Loan(s), 37, 40, 42
Loss, 31, 37–8

Madinah, 30, 44, 47–8
Maintenance support, 47, 85, 96
Makkah, 44
Māl, 19
Malthus, 65
Manīḥah, 43–4
Maqāṣid, 29, 85
Market(s), 29, 31–2, 40, 45, 67, 81; capitalism 64; demand, 29; economy, 67; forces, 28, 39, 41, 65, 67, 80–1, 86; mechanism, 7, 9, 69; structure, 31
Marx, Karl, 66–7
Masākīn, 48
Maṣlaḥah al-'āmmah, 15
Merchant(s), 62
Middle Ages, 63
Middle East, 62
Monetary policies, 29, 44, 46–7, 80–1, 86–7, 97–8
Money capital, 37–40, 84–5, 96
Mongolia, 71
Monopoly, 30, 79, 87–8
Muḍārabah, 38–9, 46
Muḥammad, the Prophet, 5–6, 15, 17–18, 26, 30–1, 33, 35, 37, 40–1, 43–4, 47, 49–51, 53, 78
Muḥtasib, 30
Muqāraḍah, 38

Mushārakah, 38
Muzāra'ah, 41

Nafaqāt, 33
Nafs, 19
Nasl, 19
Nationalization, 28, 66, 69
Needy, 6, 17–18, 42–4, 47, 49, 53, 83
Niṣāb, 50–2
North Korea, 71
Norway, 73
Nuṣūṣ, 25

Old age pensions, 69, 72
Orphan(s), 6, 36, 42, 53, 96
Ownership, 43, 68; collective, 43; private, 43; public, 68

Panel of Economists and Bankers, 8
Peasants, 63–4
Per capita income, 71, 76, 81, 98
Poor, 6, 16–17, 29, 33, 42–4, 46–50, 53, 63, 65–6, 68, 76–7, 81, 83, 88, 98
Poverty, 5–9, 11, 17, 19, 27, 43, 61, 64–7, 69–70, 72–5, 77, 80, 97; alleviation of, 48, 52, 68, 71–2, 74–5, 83; eradication of, 11, 13, 16, 21, 25, 28, 44–5, 69, 77–80, 82–4, 88, 95–8
Prayer, 5, 6
Price controls, 81
Private enterprise, 9, 27–8, 61, 95
Private property, 33–4, 43, 79
Private sector, 28
Producers, 31
Production, 38, 61, 64, 68–9, 80, 86, 95; decisions, 70; means of, 28, 37–8, 66, 79, 85, 96–7; resources, 33; state control of, 61
Profit, 37–40
Profit/loss sharing, 38, 85, 96
Profit motive, 9
Profit sharing, 37
Property, 9, 16, 27–8, 30, 32–5, 43, 96; owners, 33, 36

Qirāḍ, 38
Qur'ān, 5–6, 11, 15–21, 25–7, 29–30, 33–7, 42–4, 46–7, 49, 52, 78, 81, 84, 87–8, 96

Reform measures, 65
Rent, 37, 41, 62; of land, 40
Resources, 27, 31, 33, 45–6, 52, 64, 69–70, 86, 98
Ribā, 10
Rich, 16, 20, 32–3, 46, 53

Ṣadaqah, 42
Saving, 43
Scandinavia, 72
Securities, 50
Serfdom, 63
Share cropping, 40–1
Shares, 50
Sharī'ah, 15–16, 27, 29–30, 37–8, 40, 79, 84–5, 87
Short measurement, 31
Short weight, 31
Slavery, 62
Socialism, 7, 9, 66–7, 69–71, 79–80, 97
Social security system, 9, 18, 28, 47, 52–3, 63, 68–9, 72, 81–3, 97–8
Soviet Union, 69–70
Speenhamland Law, 65
Subsidies, 45
Sunnah, 5, 11, 15–16, 19, 21, 25–7, 29, 33, 44, 78, 84
Sweden, 73

Taḥsīniyyāt, 19, 86
Taxation, 44–5, 62, 68, 73, 83, 87, 97
Third World, 68, 73
Trade, 30, 62
Transaction(s), 31, 37, 46–7, 84
Treasury, 49

'Umar, 18
Unemployment, 17, 46–7, 65, 72, 79, 83; insurance, 9; involuntary, 29

United Kingdom, 72–3
United Nations, 77
United States of America, 64–5, 72–3, 87
'Ushr, 51

Vietnam, 71

Wages, 42, 50, 65–6, 71–2, 80
Waqf, 43
Wealth, 16, 39, 42, 48, 62, 84, 96; distribution of, 34, 88, 95
Widows, 53
World Bank, 74, 77

Yugoslavia, 70

Zakāh, 10, 18, 33, 42, 44–5, 47–52, 84, 97